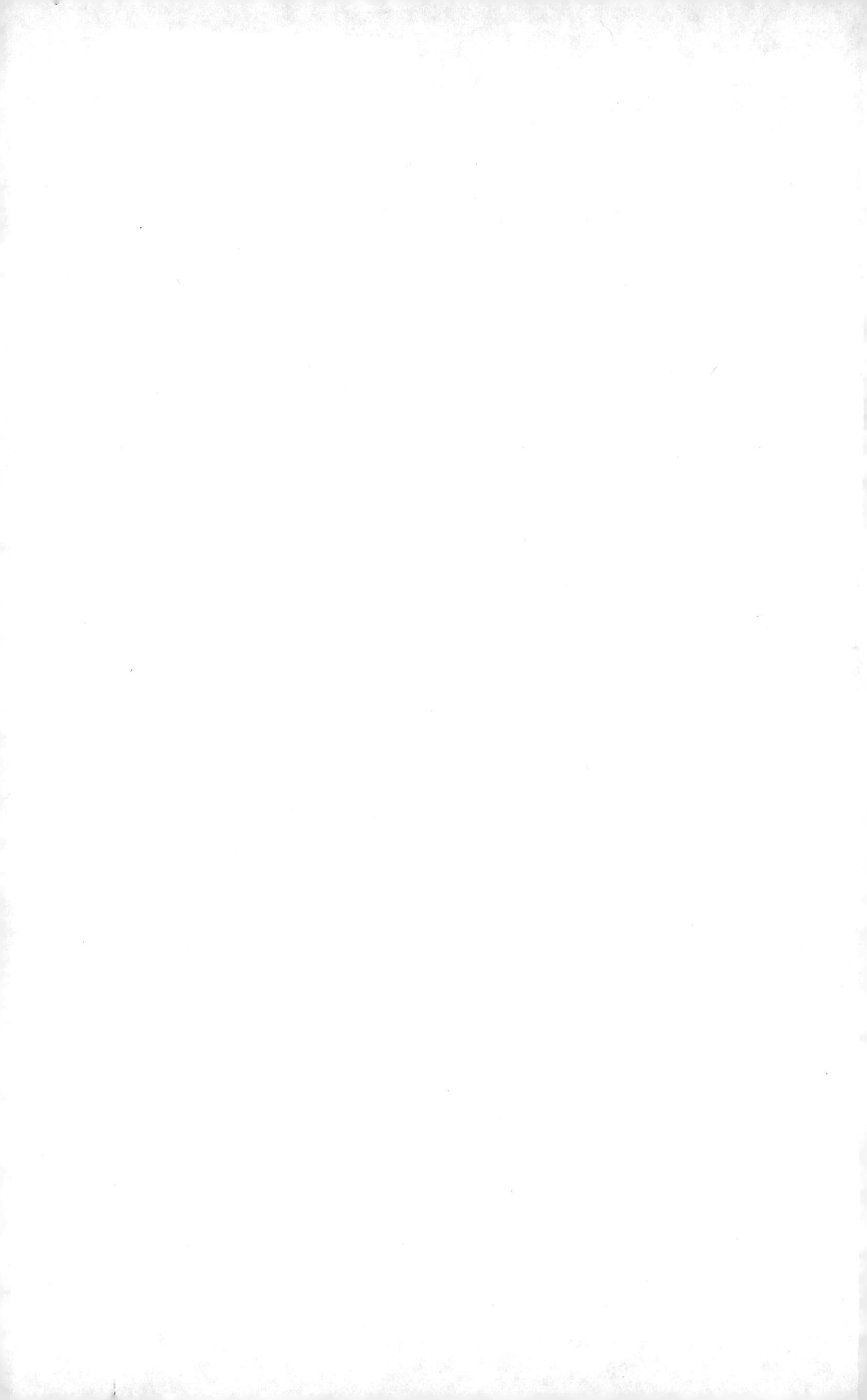

Learning By All Means:
Lessons From The Arts

PETER LANG
New York • San Francisco • Bern
Frankfurt am Main • Berlin • Wien • Paris

Learning By All Means:
Lessons From The Arts

A Study in the Philosophy of Education

V. A. Howard

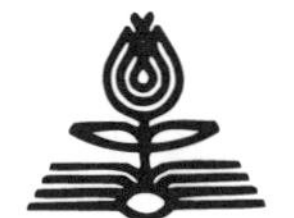

PETER LANG
New York • San Francisco • Bern
Frankfurt am Main • Berlin • Wien • Paris

Library of Congress Cataloging-in-Publication Data

Howard, V. A.
      Learning by all means : lessons from the arts : a study
in the philosophy of education / by V.A. Howard
         p. cm.
      Includes bibliographical references.
      1. Learning—Philosophy.   2. Learning, Psychology
of.   I. Title.
LB1060.H68   1992   370.15'23—dc20   91-47625
ISBN 0-8204-1570-7   CIP
ISBN 0 8204-1897-8 (pbk.)

Die Deutsche Bibliothek-CIP-Einheitsaufnahme

Howard, Vernon:
Learning by all means : lessons from the arts ; a study in the
philosophy of education / Vernon A. Howard.—New York;
Berlin; Bern; Frankfurt/M.; Paris; Wien: Lang, 1992
      ISBN 0-8204-1897-8 brosch.
      ISBN 0-8204-1570-7 Gb.

The paper in this book meets the guidelines for permanence and durability
of the Committee on Production Guidelines for
Book Longevity of the Council on Library Resources.

Contents

Acknowledgements vii

Introduction: Toward a Philosophy of Learning ix

Part I Educating the Imagination 1

1 Schiller: A Letter on Aesthetic Education to a
    Later Age 3

2 Music as Educating Imagination 9

3 Expression as Hands on Construction 27

4 One Image is Worth a Thousand Words 39

Part II Ways of Learning 59

5 Learning by Instruction 61

6 Learning by Practice 87

7 Learning by Example 109

8 Learning by Reflection 133

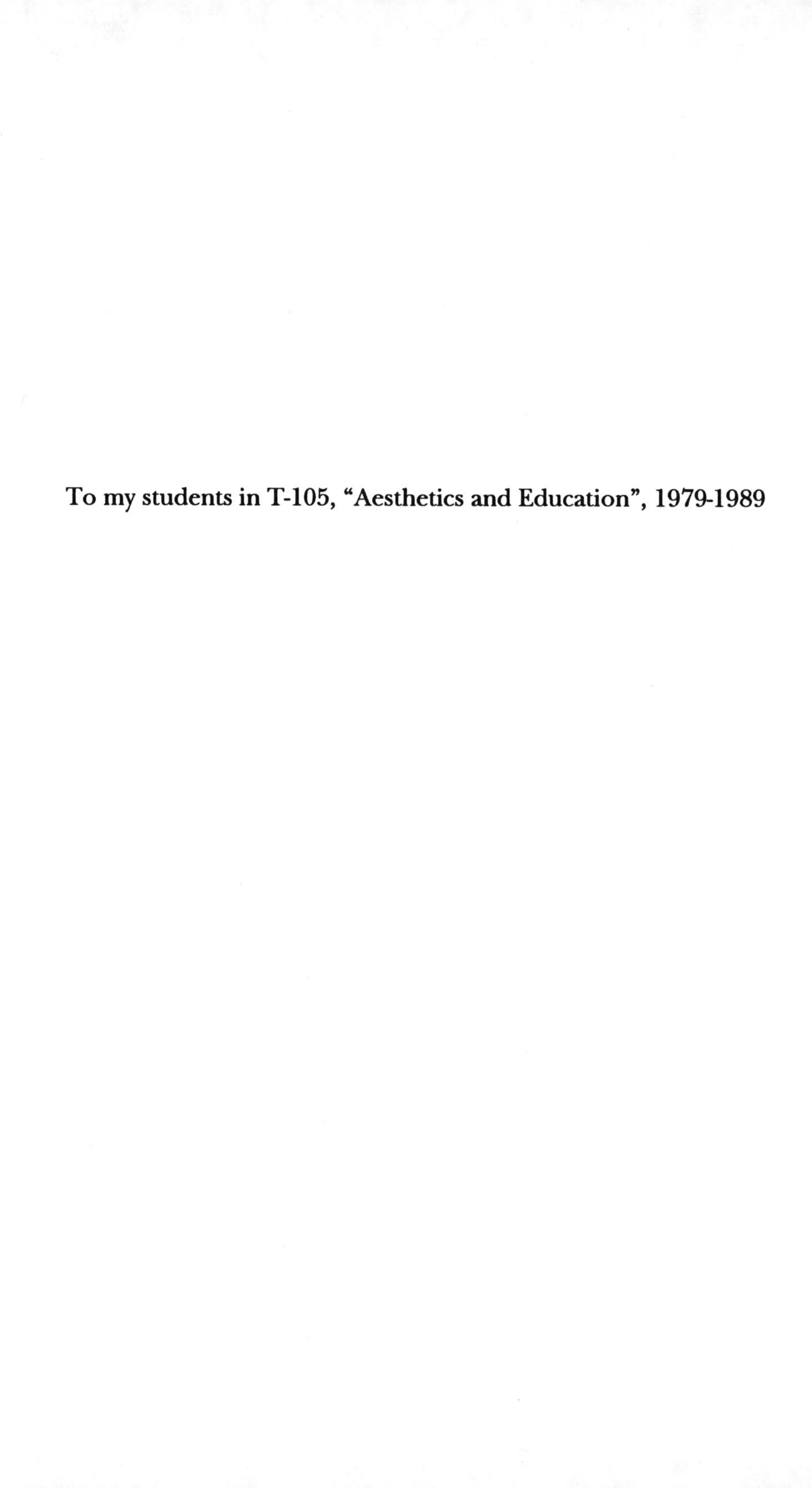

To my students in T-105, "Aesthetics and Education", 1979-1989

Acknowledgements

Being guilty, in the first instance, of writing a *philosophical* book on learning, and then, in the second, getting caught red-handed trying to fence imagination and aesthetic sensibility to learning theorists, I hesitate to acknowledge anyone for fear of incriminating them. Fortunately, I am so blatantly alone in this escapade as to be easily identified as the sole culprit responsible. Still, there are those who cannot altogether escape complicity either for having put me up to the job or for contributing details of the caper itself. Among them,

My colleagues in the Philosophy of Education Research Centre at Harvard: James H. Barton, Hanna Buczynska-Garewicz, Catherine Elgin, Kenneth Hawes, Inyhi Park, David N. Perkins, Ronald Laura, and above all, my friend, colleague, and co-director of the Centre, Israel Scheffler, whose close scrutiny of the text from first to last and many conversations on points of detail implicate him to the degree at least of being an accessory before the fact.

The Exxon Education Foundation, the John Dewey Foundation, and latterly, the Latsis Foundation, who, though not indictable on any given count, have generously fronted the whole operation.

Michael J. Flamini, Senior Acquisitions Editor, Peter Lang Publishers, Inc., who provided excellent editorial cover.

The *Journal of Aesthetic Education, The New Yorker Magazine, The Harvard Educational Review*, and the Crane Conference on Music Education who permitted me to reprint incriminating evidence.

Finally, my students in the Harvard Graduate School of Education, the guiltiest of all, who made me do it.

V. A. Howard
Deer Island, New Brunswick

Introduction:
Toward a Philosophy of Learning

O! this learning, what a thing it is.
—Shakespeare

"Ask yourself: How does a man get a 'nose' for something? And how can this nose be used?" (Wittgenstein, 1968, p. 228) Acquiring and using knowledge, how does it happen? That is the central question of learning and performance as the philosopher Wittgenstein posed it forty-odd years ago. Except for scattered remarks, he never answered it in any systematic way. Nor have philosophers since paid much attention to learning in their preoccupation with the nature of knowledge construed more as a logical product than as a mental process. Learning theory, as contrasted with theory of knowledge, has become the near exclusive preserve of psychologists; and under the towering influence of Piaget in education, learning theory in that field is virtually synonymous with child development. The adult learner of advanced skills, by whom I mean the cognitive adult—anyone over twelve years of age-gets scant attention from educational psychologists. That sometimes results in a skewed, child-centered model of learning—as if by the child's experience we may take easier measure of the adult's. (Howard, 1982, pp. 196-197)

The literature of the psychology of learning is vast. The literature of the philosophy of learning is minuscule. Many psychologists among behaviorists, cognitivists, or gestaltists, including clinicians, would own up to being learning theorists. Hardly any philosophers would accept the label. Appropriately enough, John Dewey in large portions of his work may be the only major philosophical figure of the twentieth century actually to *fit* the label.

Not even the philosophers of education have pursued the nature of learning and skilled performance with the same zeal with which they have pursued the kindred topics of teaching, curriculum, the conditions and forms of knowledge, the aims and concepts of education. That may be a matter of disciplinary discretion, of conceding the supposedly "empirical" questions of when and how we learn to cognitive science while maintaining hegemony over the epistemological and normative issues of what we learn and why. But I would say that how, what, when, and why we learn are as much philosophical as psychological questions throughout. Neither discipline, by virtue of methodology alone, can lay claim to exclusive ownership of such basic questions of learning. Both have much to contribute to them all.

The past twenty years have seen a renewed interest on the part of some psychologists in the philosophical aspects of learning theory. One thinks again of Piaget who fancied himself a genetic *epistemologist*, certainly of Chomsky (1966) in psycholinguistics; but more recently, of the work of Jerome Bruner (1986), Howard Gardner (1983), David N. Perkins (1981), and the late Paul Kolers (1972)—all of them influenced by the philosopher Nelson Goodman's theories of perception and symbolism. (Goodman, 1972, 1977, 1984)

But where are the philosophers? Goodman himself could hardly be described as a philosopher of learning notwithstanding his many contributions to the theory of symbols, epistemology, and aesthetics. Even the philosophers of education, John Passmore (1981), R. S. Peters (1959, 1966) and Israel Scheffler (1960, 1973), not to mention a host of others, deal with learning in ways mostly ancillary to questions of teaching, curriculum, schooling, and the aims and values of education. A noteworthy exception is Maxine Greene's perceptive study, *Landscapes of Learning* (1978): but her focus is more in the direction of the social philosophy of learning than on learning theory as such.

Of the aforementioned, Scheffler comes closest to suggesting the lineaments of a philosophic theory of learning, particularly in his studies of metaphor and of human potential (1979, 1985; see also my review of the former, Howard, 1981). Yet one does not think of a Passmore, a Peters, or even a Scheffler laying special claim to the title, "Learning Theorist of Philosophical Ilk", despite their many careful analyses of the conceptual topography that includes learning. Broadly speaking, they are more concerned with the language of education, education's inherent assumptions, values, and guiding conceptions than with specific kinds of learning, the pattern of their interrelationships, and how they work. Still less are they concerned with the failures of learning, the frustrations, and the personal struggles of learning that figure prominently in the experience of individuals.

Two notable exceptions fore and aft of Wittgenstein come to mind as having constructed full fledged philosophic theories of learning: John Dewey, as mentioned, and Michael Polanyi, the chemist turned philosopher, neither of whom adopted the label for those parts of their work which it fits. Dewey, of course, wrote about everything educational, but I have in mind especially his early *Democracy and Education* (1916); and later, *How We Think* (1933); and *Art as Experience* (1934). In all these works, learning, as a critical and "aesthetic" activity—one that engages the individual's mind, body, and sensibilities simultaneously—is in the forefront. [1]

What is a philosophical theory of learning about? How does it differ from epistemology or theory of knowledge? In *Personal Knowledge*, Polanyi speaks of the "personalisation" of knowledge, distinguishing what is known about a subject from what we as individuals know and how. (Polanyi, 1958, pp. 16-17) In a similar vein, Gilbert Ryle speculates in passing towards the end of *The Concept of Mind* that the phrase "theory of knowledge" may refer to either the products or to the processes of inquiry: to either "the structures of built theories" or to "the theory of learning, discovery and invention". (Ryle, 1949, p. 317) The latter, he surmises, is a "theory of getting to know . . . concerned with the terms in which certain episodes in the lives of individuals are described and prescribed for by teachers and examiners". (p. 318)

Such "terms" encompass various modes of instruction by direction and explanation, by tests and criticism, by practice and drill, by rules and routines, by hints and cues, by demonstrations and examples, by imitation and copying—all aimed at understanding something, getting the "sense" or "hang" of it, a "nose" for it, as we say, or the right feel for a skill or performance. Such comprehension, intellectual or physical, artistic or scientific, theoretical or practical, is mediated by a variety of symbolic systems requiring *interpretation* through many phases of a growing understanding.

The domain of "getting to know" is one that Dewey describes as "the organic connection between education and personal experience". (Dewey, 1938, p. 25) "Personal experience" here I take to cover a wide range of learning experiences from acquiring trained capacities and skills, like multiplication or keyboard technique, to the higher reaches of mathematical reasoning or musical performance. And the "organic connection" I take to refer to self involvement with the task at hand, to self criticism, and to self discipline. The specific focus, then, of a philosophy of learning is on the instructional (including self instructional) efforts of mind and body that culminate in one's saying, "I've got it!", "I understand now", "I can do it", "I can go on from here". (Cf. Wittgenstein, 1968, p. 60)

How does this differ from psychological learning theories? Mainly, I think, in focussing upon the logical conditions, the conceptual topography, and mental activities, the symbolic structures, instructional means, controlling values, and specific objectives that sustain learning at any given time, in any given area. In short, the philosophy of learning sketches the odyssey of personal and public achievement anywhere learning occurs.

That emphasis contrasts with the specialized taxonomies, controlled experiments, and formal theories of the psychology of learning, less in opposition than complementary to the latter. The psychological literature mostly dwells upon learning rates, behavioural changes (e.g., schedules of reinforcement), learning "plateaus" and "styles", on the one hand, and upon the sequences or "stages" of cognitive (including moral and aesthetic) development, on the other. A philosophy of learning looks at learning as it happens in particular cases and asks, How is this possible?

Notwithstanding their different emphases, the philosophy and psychology of learning are contiguous, and, at times, overlapping enterprises—particularly on questions of perception, meaning, values, culture, creativity, and symbolism. They cannot escape each other bound as they are by tradition and common concerns. Collaborative research on these and allied topics is already a reality in some quarters. [2]

Comprising the domain of "getting to know" are the rationales, procedures, symbolic systems, explanations, and tests of competence used by persons in quest of understanding or expertise. That is the area I shall be exploring herein on a small scale with primary emphasis upon learning in the arts. Accordingly, I should not be averse to describing this study as an exercise in *practical* philosophy in the way Stephen Toulmin uses the term to refer to "the issues arising out of the clinical aspects of medicine, the procedures and practices of law, the rhetorical force of personal argumentation, and the moral methods of the casuists". (Toulmin, 1988, p. 341) My concern is with the "clinical aspects" of learning and of education generally.[3] Similarly, a psychologist reader of these pages[4], noting the emphasis upon mental and physical process (*versus* product), subsumed the whole under the general label, *a philosophy of human performance*. Admittedly, in method and content this is a hybrid work requiring some negative as well as positive delineation.

What, therefore, I shall *not* be doing is constructing a "grand theory" of learning out of what goes on in the arts notwithstanding the generality of the discussion. While the arts, particularly the performing arts, will serve as principal sources of examples and direction, the issues involved have their analogues elsewhere: in craft, technology, the professions, and science, and I shall be mindful of them wherever possible. Would that I *could* illuminate the entire landscape of learning and human performance in all these areas, but that is asking too much of a small book. Fortunately, the terrain of the arts overlaps the others enough to suggest future explorations beyond those undertaken here. In a word, first things first, from a philosophical point of view.

The Task

In *Artistry: the Work of Artists* (1982), I examined some of the functions of technical languages with special reference to the arts focussing upon the relations of craft to art; the relations of practical to theoretical knowledge; the roles of creativity and imagination in the growth of performance skills; the varieties, levels, and interrelations of skill and understanding; and the types of thinking and awareness involved in different sorts of practice and drill. Some passing attention was given to how standards are developed and deployed through the passage from base competency to mastery. (See Howard, 1982, pp. 144ff)

Here I especially want to expand upon the latter theme of the whence and whither of standards in learning experience—in other words, the place of controlling values in learning to learn: where they come from; how we "internalise" them; what changes they undergo with the growth of competence; how they may help or hinder progress; how they shape critical judgement and practice; how they shape the nature of the task itself; and, perhaps most importantly, how they shape the ways we come to identify *with* the task.

Cutting across the many ways of learning, I see imagination as playing a crucial role, less as a matter of inspiration than of aspiration, as an element of control holding ends-in-view while also revising them relative to what next we want to accomplish. Imagination is the meeting place of past and present experience, of memory and anticipation—a place of "silent rehearsal" and assessment—from which may emerge new directions for future efforts.

With due regard for the many meanings attached to the word 'imagination' (Ryle, 1949, pp. 245-279; Howard, 1982, pp. 136-148), my tentative view is that a growth of critical judgement requires a corresponding growth of imagination regarding what next is practically feasible—in effect, what *can* be, what *might* be discovered or done. Ingredient to that growth of critical judgement is imagination's role in establishing and sustaining the overall direction of trial and error practice where one facility embeds within another, e.g., learning to play the piano or mastering laboratory procedures. All that I describe here stands in marked contrast to two extremes: drudgery, on the one hand, or means without dreams; and fantasy, on the other, or dreams without means. My purpose overall is to show how means and dreams get connected.

Central also to a philosophy of learning is the notion of skill. And central to *acquiring* most skills is the issue, once again, of interpretation; of how instructions and tasks are to be construed, practiced, carried forward. How one does that, I am convinced, depends at least partly on what one thinks skills to be. Are they simple matters of routine? Are they learned by sheer drill? What about complex skills where judgement and choice are involved in their deployment, as in law, medicine, or teaching? What standards and values are reflected in these different conceptions of skill? Where and how do questions of character and of identification with the task at hand come to bear upon one's ability to learn; to endure harsh criticism or to persist in the face of failure?

The foregoing is a sampling of the topics and questions considered herein. Generally, my procedure is to root the discussion in particular examples of learning: by doing as one is told or instructed to do, by cultivating certain habits of discrimination and observation, by taking chances and reviewing the consequences, by pursuing an ideal, by surviving in demanding circumstances, by painstaking effort, by practice. In short, I shall be worrying the old cliché about what it is to learn how to learn.

Origins and Overview of the Book

Much of this book is influenced by my teaching over the past ten years in the Harvard Graduate School of Education, particularly a course called, "Aesthetics and Education" (T-105), designed for students interested in arts education: musicians, painters, teachers of English and drama, arts administrators, museum personnel, art therapists, and the like. One of their recurrent questions is, What is this thing called "aesthetic education"? With a host of books, national reports, and even a journal sporting the label, I felt obliged to come to terms with the notion. To do that, I went back to one of the original sources, Friedrich Schiller's *Letters on the Aesthetic Education of Man* (1795).

Schiller's neo-Kantian vocabulary and eighteenth century poetic style are tough going for nonphilosophers, and the *Letters* are seldom cited in the literature on aesthetic education. Yet I am persuaded that no better statement exists of what aesthetic education is, including its relations to the moral and social realms, and its role in individual learning and development. Moreover, Schiller's notion of aesthetic education is by no means confined to the arts, but rather concerns the cultivation of taste and judgement in virtually any domain of learning.

To assist my students, and to establish a general background for discussion of learning and teaching in the arts, I tried writing a *prolegomenon* to Schiller's *Letters* in modern prose. That was unsuccessful for the reason that his thought is so wrapped up in the philosophic and poetic idioms of his time. My effort simply lacked the feel of the *Letters*. So instead I undertook to write a reenactment, a compendium, of Schiller's *Letters* working from the original German and English translation in the form of what I imagined he might have wanted to say to the future. The result is Chapter 1, "Schiller: A Letter on Aesthetic Education to a Later Age". Weaving together whole bits of Schiller's prose and my own fabrications, this fictional "last Letter" represents an explication and interpretation (*cum* defense) of Schiller's vision of aesthetic education in brief compass. I include it here, as in my class, to set the stage for the analyses of learning to follow. In the last Chapter, "Learning by Reflection", I again take up Schiller's main idea, transmitted through Dewey and others, of the unity of sensibility and understanding in learning experience.

Part I, "Educating the Imagination", mostly dwells upon the ways in which imagination gets developed and used in highly disciplined yet creative ways in and by the arts (Chapter 2). Of special note in this connection are the ways artists learn to find self expression through works of art (Chapter 3). Again, the examples chosen are mostly musical, but the intent is quite general as will be evident. Part I concludes by confronting the controversy in philosophy and psychology over the status of mental imagery in learning with suggestions for how talk of "mental pictures" is to be understood practically and theoretically (Chapter 4). While the technical issues of imagery are vital to the aforementioned rapprochement between the philosophy and psychology of learning, the general reader need not be deterred by them. Still, I would hope that even a cursory reading would be sufficient to catch the drift of that intriguing dialogue of the disciplines.

Part II, "Ways of Learning", examines the roles of imagination, inquiry, and symbolism in typical learning situations including self-teaching experiences, by explicit instruction (Chapter 5), by practice (Chapter 6), by example (Chapter 7), and by reflection (Chapter 8). Throughout, the spotlight is on the interpretive activities of the learner and the wide range of symbols required to achieve a proper "reading" (or any reading, for that matter) of what is to be learned. As well, the topography of skill is revisited in these chapters with special regard for those all important lessons from failure where means and dreams fall apart and frustration tests our patience.

Notes

1 Like William James, Dewey straddled psychology and philosophy, daring to speak substantively in either voice. Inevitably, as the two disciplines went their separate ways between the wars and thereafter, specialists in both fields fled each others' company methodologically. That partly accounts for how knowledge (as a logical matter) got left to the philosophers while learning, or "knowing" (as an empirical matter) went with the psychologists.

2 I have in mind the multi-disciplinary work of Harvard Project Zero in the arts, of the Project on Human Potential at Harvard, of the Institute for Logic & Cognitive Studies at The University of Houston - Clear Lake, and of the Philosophy of Education Research Centre at Harvard.

3 According to Toulmin, " . . . philosophy displays a series of historical pendulum swings between two broad agendas. On one agenda, the task of philosophy is to say whatever can be said in any field of inquiry that is entirely general; on the other ["practical"] agenda, the task is to say whatever can be said that is as general as the field permits". (Toulmin, 1988, p. 348)

4 Dr. Scott Frazier whose shrewd methodological observations helped me to clarify the approach taken herein.

References

Jerome Bruner, *Actual Minds, Possible Worlds* (Cambridge: Harvard University Press, 1986).

Noam Chomsky, *Cartesian Linguistics, a Chapter in the History of Rationalist Thought* (New York: Harper and Row, 1966).

John Dewey, *Democracy and Education* (New York: Macmillan, 1966); first published in 1916.

John Dewey, *How we Think: A Restatement of the Relation of Reflective Thinking to the Educative Process* (Carbondale: University of Southern Illinois Press, 1985); first published in 1933.

John Dewey, *Art as Experience* (New York: Putnam, 1958); first published in 1934.

John Dewey, *Experience and Education* (New York: Collier, 1963); first published in 1938.

Howard Gardner, *Frames of Mind* (New York: Basic Books, 1983).

Nelson Goodman, *Languages of Art, An Approach to a Theory of Symbols* (Indianapolis: Hackett, 1972).

Nelson Goodman, *The Structure of Appearance*, 3rd edition, (Dordrect: Reidel, 1977).

Nelson Goodman, *Of Mind and Other Matters* (Cambridge: Harvard University Press, 1984).

Maxine Greene, *Landscapes of Learning* (New York: Teachers College Press, 1975).

D. W. Hamlyn, "Logical and Psychological Aspects of Learning", in R. S. Peters (ed.) *The Concept of Education* (London: Routledge & Kegan Paul, 1967).

V. A. Howard, Review of Israel Scheffler, *Beyond the Letter, A Philosophical Inquiry into Ambiguity, Vagueness, and Metaphor in Language*, in *Harvard Educational Review*, vol. 51, no. 3, August 1981.

V. A. Howard, *Artistry: the Work of Artists* (Indianapolis: Hackett, 1982).

Paul Kolers, *Aspects of Motion Perception* (Oxford: Pergamon, 1979).

John Passmore, *The Philosophy of Teaching* (Cambridge: Harvard University Press, 1980).

David N. Perkins, *The Mind's Best Work* (Cambridge: Harvard University Press, 1981).

R. S. Peters, *Authority, Responsibility, and Education* (London: Allen & Unwin, 1959).

R. S. Peters, *Ethics and Education* (London: Allen & Unwin, 1966).

Michael Polanyi, *Personal Knowledge: Towards a Post-Critical Philosophy* (London: Routledge & Kegan Paul, 1958).

Gilbert Ryle, *The Concept of Mind* (Chicago: University of Chicago Press, 1984); first published in 1949.

Israel Scheffler, *The Language of Education* (Springfield: Charles C. Thomas, 1960).

Israel Scheffler, *Conditions of Knowledge* (Chicago: University of Chicago Press, 1986); first published in 1965.

Israel Scheffler, *Reason and Teaching* (London: Routledge & Kegan Paul, 1973).

Israel Scheffler, *Beyond the Letter, A Philosophical Inquiry into Ambiguity, Vagueness, and Metaphor in Language* (London: Routledge & Kegan Paul, 1979).

Israel Scheffler, *Of Human Potential* (London: Routledge & Kegan Paul, 1985).

Friedrich Schiller, *On the Aesthetic Education of Man, in a Series of Letters*, (tr.) Reginald Snell (New York: Fredrick Ungar, 1965); original German text published in 1795.

Stephen Toulmin, "The Recovery of Practical Philosophy", *The American Scholar*, Summer 1988, pp. 337-352.

Ludwig Wittgenstein, *Philosophical Investigations*, (tr.) G. E. M. Anscombe (Oxford: Blackwell, 1976); first published in 1953.

PART I

EDUCATING THE IMAGINATION

1

Schiller: A Letter on Aesthetic Education to a Later Age

Enacted and Annotated by V. A. Howard

Ars longa, vita brevis
—Hippocrates

If I should not care to be living in another century, or to have laboured for another, I am nonetheless confident that the *ideas* predominant in my *Letters*, stripped of their technicalities and philosophical variances, will emerge as the consensus of mankind in regard to matters of education and the refinement of sensibility. The sorry skeleton of my words discloses but a fleeting appearance of the living Truth bequeathed by that moral instinct by which Nature guides Man to maturity. It is perhaps admissible then, that I should in this last letter address a later age, some two hundred years hence, when, as I surmise, mankind will have advanced further toward that pinnacle of Beauty which alone can unite his soul and his society.

Since the conflagration that consumed the originals of my *Letters* (in a fire in 1794 at the palace of Prince Friedrich Christian of Denmark at whose behest I wrote them) I cannot assure their material survival much less their survival in the memory of an enlightened age for whom they will be but the residue of a worried past. Yet I presume to engage your free intellectual powers—our common endowment—in brief compass in order to elucidate, as best my Art and manner permit, the primary element of Play, *spieltrieb*, in the aesthetic education of ideal human nature.

No doubt, a new Science of mind will supplant in detail if not in spirit the *critical* philosophy which led empiricism back to principle and speculation back to experience and myself to aver character at the heart of all that deserves to be called education, since the way to the head must lie through the heart. Nourished in my views by the milk of a better age and by unsurpassed philosophic and poetic genius in my own, I ventured in my previous *Letters* to delineate a view of Man now divided against himself, lacerated by his special achievements, fragmented, with the noise of the wheel he drives everlastingly in his ears; and over all, a State urging him to bring in honour and profit.

All that stands in opposition to what Man can and should be. And so I beg your indulgence, in deference to past hopes, for this rehearsal of a psychology born at once out of a darkening age and an inquiring heart. Withal, my private pursuit is to illuminate in some small measure further to my original *Letters* the vocation of Man: his genius for Play.

My earlier reposte to those who would place Freedom, especially political freedom, before Beauty in the quest for human improvement was that in practice we can learn to serve Freedom honestly and faithfully only if we first learn to serve Beauty; that the moral condition can be developed only from the aesthetic, not from the physical condition.

If this appears an onerous burden to place on aesthetic culture, it was civilized culture itself that inflicted upon us the wound of detachment of our mental faculties; first by the intricate machinery of States with their attendant dissociations of ranks and occupations, and then by the sharper divisions of the sciences. Who in the unforgiving moment could foresee that an enlarged experience and the greater dominance of Utility would erode the essential bond of human nature and set in its place a ruinous conflict of our sensuous and rational impulses? But so it has been, and, as I exactly said, must be for any people at all that is in process of civilisation, since all without distinction must fall away from Nature through over-subtlety of intellect before they can return to her through Reason.

Reason reveals by dissection, by laying bare the several functions of parts that contribute to the concert, or discord, of the organism as a whole. Applied to the nature of Mind, reason reveals mankind as caught up in a contest, psychologically and historically, between two warring impulses: the material or sensuous impulse, *stopftrieb*, and the rational or formal impulse, *formtrieb*. The one represents feeling, intuition, sensation, and immediacy; the other, thought, judgement, law, and eternity; the one the life of the natural, unfettered man, the other the life of the principled, restrained man. Each taken by itself represents an extreme *within* us: the sensuous impulse gives us the moment, sensation, the diversity of experience; the formal impulse gives us law, judgement, and the continuity of the person through experience. Only as Man alters does he *exist*; only as he remains unalterable does *he* exist.

A person is necessarily compounded of such unity in diversity—of a self that persists through change. As with any healthy organism, it is not a question of the dominion of one function over another, or of artificially or forcibly closing the gap between functions that tend in opposite directions. Rather, a third, supervenient function is required that synthesizes even as it orchestrates the several functions of mind and body. That is the aesthetic impulse, *spieltrieb*, the sense of Beauty, what otherwise in its practical activity of harmonious mediation I call Play. At this juncture I can only repeat the central question of my earlier *Letters*; namely, how is it reasonable to expect from aesthetic sensibility, from Play, so great a result as the education of humanity?

Let us reflect now upon our intelligent faculties relative to our condition. Throughout the persistence of the person the condition changes, through every change of condition the person persists. Such unity of mind in no wise contradicts the indwelling of the two fundamental impulses striving for their separate objectives. Will—our ability to deliberate and to choose—holds authority over them both, neither of which can act in direct authority over the other. Not by the most high minded principles is the violent man restrained from injustice nor the principled man led to injustice by temptation except as each chooses to act one way or the other.

Neither, however, is the unity of Mind a mere sum total or compound of physical, rational, and moral determinations. The sensuous impulse awakens earliest with the primal experience of life followed by the rational impulse with the experience of law and the beginning of personality; just then, when both impulses are in place, is Man's humanity fully established, and accordingly, his capacity for freedom and moral choice.

Simultaneously our condition becomes richly variegated. Phenomena present themselves to our sensuous natures as related to our well being; to our rational natures as giving us knowledge; and to our deliberating natures as matters of rational, moral choice. Yet only as things appear to us in the *unity* of their physical, logical, and moral characters are they viewed contemplatively—as aesthetic. So as I wrote in my *Letters*, there is an education for understanding, an education for morality, and an education for taste. The latter alone has as its aim the cultivation of the whole of our sensuous and intellectual powers in the fullest possible harmony.

Precisely as things appear to us in their various aspects, as our faculties are activated together in harmonious concert, the Mind begins to play, to synthesize reason and sensation, thought and feeling, law and freedom in a living form, *lebensform*. Living form denotes the aesthetic qualities of all phenomena—or Beauty in the widest sense.

Yet the question remains *how* to educate for taste building upon the capacity for Play. And here I beg to post an addendum to my *Letters* in plain, practical terms. Again, I am confident of that unbroken thread of enlightened opinion stretching from antiquity to my own day and beyond.

To make Beauty from beautiful objects is the task of aesthetic education. In so saying I mean that training in the Fine Arts is less an end in itself than a tutelage of the sensibilities by examples, by presenting the mind with occasions for contemplation of a sort that enlivens the imagination in all its realms: from poetry to science to politics. Pedagogically, we find in Fine Art that "right measure" of intellect and sensibility so admired by the Greeks as a condition simultaneously of personal integration and social harmony. Still, as instructive as fine art can be, there is no place in true education for instructive art in any partisan sense. A didactic, moralistic art is self-contradictory, being at odds with the concept of Play which can never have a tendentious effect upon the improvement of character.

My detractors complain that I confound Play as a means of uniting the sensuous and rational impulses with Play as a constituent of the highest forms of rational life. I do, but deliberately; for the means merge with the ends in all true education. When I said that there is no other way to make the sensuous man rational than by first making him aesthetic, I meant to convey that the aesthetic as a *via media* becomes contained within the rational man as an achievement, softening him sufficiently to adjust his principles to *cases*, allowing him to temper his judgement. In the matter of developing taste and judgement, there is no line to be drawn: the means of transition, of tutelage, blend with character at every stage.

It is never a question whether we shall have taste; it is always a question what we shall do to improve it. In no wise do I view the aesthetic condition as an absolute; for its mechanism can be used against our best interests, for example, to persuade us to injustice where reason is in eclipse. Thought needs a body and form can only be realized in some material. Accordingly, the aesthetic condition is supervenient upon the spontaneity of reason and sense enhancing their function by a superior judgement in human and scientific affairs.

Play, I must insist, is never trivial. The balance of freedom and rule, of joy and restraint as evident in games and sport is all one with the agility and speed of intellect in its highest reaches; for as intellect meets with perception, necessity puts aside its seriousness, because it grows *light*. A joy of discovery, of surprise, enlivens our most somber inquiries. Man must needs keep before him his games as reminders; for if he is serious with the agreeable, the comprehensible, and the good, with Beauty he plays. Which is to say, he resolves a tension and achieves a state of equipoise, a subtle balance between tension and release, in effect, a discipline of expression of a kind familiar to performing artists—an artistry of living and of inquiry. That is aesthetic education.

In concluding my epistle to a later age, I humbly beseech you as I did my Lord and patron in the ninth of my *Letters*: Live with your century, but do not be its creature; render to your contemporaries what they need, not what they praise . . . Think of them as they ought to be when you have to influence them, but think of them as they are when you are tempted to act on their behalf.

References

Friedrich von Schiller, *On the Aesthetic Education of Man, in a Series of Letters*, tr. Reginald Snell (New York, Frederick Ungar, 1965); original German text published in 1795.

nagination

Imaginal Controls

Let us consider the Janus faced question: how is imagination involved in learning to appreciate and to perform music; and what does such learning contribute to the discipline of the imagination generally? In other words, how is imagination involved in musical training in ways kindred to other disciplined activities?

The key word here is 'discipline' and only then 'imagination'; for while my immediate focus is on the connections among learning, thinking, and doing in performance, the larger context is the whole of that seemingly inarticulate side of human intelligence—craft, skill, technique, practice, mastery and artistry, with special attention to their critical and imaginative dimensions.

By no means am I suggesting that musical training is somehow "good" for something else. Rather, my objective is to place music education squarely within the domain not only of art education, but of liberal education by examining certain mental processes ingredient to it. A secondary objective is to indicate how music, through its personal and public meanings, contributes to the growth of understanding. En route I shall fire a broad side or two at the "creativity" and "critical thinking" movements in education studies.

None of these matters will receive the wealth of analysis and argumentation they deserve. Elsewhere (Howard, 1982), I have pursued in fair detail the topic of artistry in performance and partly directs the effort. Mme. Nilsson's instruction to imagine that one is smelling a flower in the production of a vocal sound is an example of what I call *heuristic imagination*, to distinguish it from other varieties. (Howard, 1982, pp. 136-139)

Other examples of heuristic imagination include such familiar phenomena as "mental rehearsal": going over things "in the mind's eye" before or after doing them; forming or holding particular ends-in-view such as the visual image of a shape one wishes to draw, the aural image of a desired sound, a game plan, or correction to be made in practice; metaphoric imagery—"Imagine the throat as a tall dome across which the voice travels", "Imagine that you are ascending and descending a plumb line in executing the plié"; and aspect perception—the flow of colours in a Renoir, the face in the clouds, the hidden fifth in a musical progression. In these and many other ways, mental imagery constitutes a "mind set" or selective predilection to specific patterns of thought, action, and perception.

The kind of useful imaginings alluded to above are of a sort Dewey describes as "a way of seeing and feeling things as they compose an integral whole. [Recall Mr. Barth's sudden "understanding" above.] It is the large and generous blending of interests at the point where the mind comes in contact with the world. [Often through effort, failure, or success.] When old and familiar things are made new in experience, there is imagination." (Dewey, 1958, p. 267)

To repeat, what is imagination's function in the growth of performing judgement? Four uses of imagination are particularly worthy of mention here not only for their musical significance but for their importance to learning in general. The imagination can be used to mediate between ends and means, to hold the vision of a final product in view, to promote a spirit of inquiry, and to enhance personal standards of performance.

Useful Imaginings

A primary use of imagination is as mediator between means and ends. Seldom do we learn anything so complex as playing a musical instrument or interpreting music in a fixed and final way. Both technical and interpretative abilities admit of indefinite refinement. Technical skills cultivated by drill are embedded within higher level capacities requiring constant attention to detail, judgement, and choice. And even drill, at *some* point requires close scrutiny of how exercises are to be done, what constitutes correct performance of them, and why one does them. Ultimately, such diagnostic judgement is a matter of calibrating techniques and skills already mastered to ever changing circumstances and new performance demands. Only thus, for instance, was Mr. Barth able to make the sudden leap of understanding to a better level of performance using abilities already in hand. Similarly, the soprano singing Micaela's aria is shown how to transform the fear she feels into expressive power.

The estrangement of means and ends is a double estrangement: of means without ends (drudgery) or of ends without means (fantasy), neither of which is the name of success. In imagination we learn to connect them up in ways that enable us to realize our dreams. That in turn requires a discipline of the mind as much as of the body through practice. To parody Kant, imagination without practice is empty; practice without imagination is blind.

A second, and even more fundamental, use of imagination in performance is to hold ends-in-view within a continuum of ends and means. What that Deweyean mouthful means is that our performance techniques and objectives co-vary under the pressure of changes and challenges foreseen and unforeseen. Means and ends require continual, *mutual* reevaluation as one's abilities and understanding grow. Or, to put it another way, our original performance objectives change as our facilities to realize them improve. (Cf. Dewey, 1972, pp. 45-47) Improved facility at the keyboard, for example, enables one not only to perform a musical passage up to some preconceived standard of phraseology, but to reconceive the phraseology itself—to project a new standard.

Ends and means-in-view can both be proximate or final: building facilities like keyboard fluency or performing publicly up to or beyond standard, finger drill or dress rehearsal. But only as ends and means are "taken in", made part of one's intelligent response repertoire, do they form a *continuum*; that is, escape being mere rote responses or a "bag of tricks".

With the exceptions of commands, recipes, and drill manuals, ends and their means-in-view are not simply read off from either tradition or from the situation at hand. Rather, they are held in imagination as directives (rules and routines) and frequently revised therein as changing circumstances demand. In effect, imagination allows us to adjust our acquired know-how and techniques to particular cases and even to revise them or transfer them to new realms of application. (Howard, 1982, p. 135)

A third function of the imagination in performance is to promote a spirit of inquiry: to enable us to change our course of action according to what we learn from our mistakes; in other words, to revise. Even the humblest finger drills are trial and error "experiments" the significance of which is entirely lost if we cannot measure our mistakes against our goals. Nothing in the behaviour itself tells us what we *ought* to be doing or how. Rather, the remembrance of things just past is held up in comparison to the desired ideal, with the aim of closing the gap through successive approximations, as something possible to do.

Part of the essential discipline of practice is to remember and to compare ruthlessly trial after trial by reference to a standard clearly conceived—in effect to *take care*. It takes time and much effort to learn how to care in the sense of critically heeding one's moment to moment efforts. Yet such caring is the first lesson of practice for without it, practice degenerates into mere repetition or drudgery without correction or direction. (Howard, 1982, pp. 160-164) The implicit distinction here is between critical foresight and mere preconception or slavish adherence to habit or routine. Only in imagination can we confront past experience with present challenge by holding ends *in* view as well as the past in *re*-view. In so doing, imagination focusses the whence and the whither of our efforts in critical overview, supporting the will by showing a way.

Finally, imagination plays a crucial role in the assimilation and growth of personal standards of performance. It's easy to admire virtuosity at a distance in blissful ignorance of what makes it possible (a prime source, incidentally, of appeals to amorphous "creativity", "inspiration", "gifts", "talent", and the like). It's far more difficult to understand it, or to take such virtuosity as a personal goal, break it down into digestible bits, and to "keep the flame" while enduring all the pain. In *Artistry* I half humorously described such an apprenticeship as follows.

> Nearly anyone who takes the trouble to look into this book can recollect labours of love or loathing at the keyboard, at the drawing board, in the exercise studio, or on the playing field. The sheer drudgery of it all as measured against the evolving vision of mastery is perhaps one of the most daunting, humbling experiences known to us. Long periods of Sisyphean despair punctuated at intervals by the elation of small accomplishments, the wagering of one's talents against the odds of perfection, the feeling that pain and failure are one's only reliable companions, such are the moods of ambition when subjected to a hard discipline. The pathos of the quest for mastery is amusingly captured in baritone Louis Quilico's mock prayer: "Dear God, you gave me a voice. I didn't ask for it. So help me!" At the opposite extreme, one imagines another version: "Dear God, I asked for a voice. You didn't give it to me. So help me to practice!" Whatever the speed of learning or the proportion of one's "gifts", the fact of practice—the necessity of honing one's talents—remains. (p. 157)

And I would go further: whether we are concerned with music "appreciation" or conservatory training, one equation remains constant: namely, that the *ideas* and the *ideals* of music (or of virtually anything worth learning, for that matter) go hand in glove. It's what we refer to colloquially as "getting the feel" or "the hang" of something, albeit a slice of performance strategy, a sense of what is going on in opera, or, equally important, a feel for the appropriate methods of inquiry into such matters.

To develop such "feeling", it is not enough to learn the skills and techniques of inquiry or of performance alone. To be able is not necessarily to be willing, or conversely. (Cf. Scheffler, 1965, pp. 19-20) One needs also to acquire the *disposition* to use the techniques of inquiry or performance. That is what it means to connect means to ends-in-view. It is a question not only of identifying the task but of identifying with it.

Now it is far easier to teach definite skills than it is to teach dispositions, just as it is easier to teach someone how to balance a chequebook than to inculcate the value of thrift. (The example is Scheffler's, 1965, p. 19) The one is a question of particular facilities, the other of character and personality. Yet both are required if learning in any domain is to be more than a futile exercise. But how are dispositions, the *values* and *ideals* of a discipline, taught?

I am tempted here to take the Socratic way out and say that they cannot be taught, not because they aren't learnt somehow, nor because they are unspecifiable, but because they have to be felt and absorbed as *aspirations* as well as known. That is the "aesthetic" face of all sustained learning and inquiry: the personal thrill of achievement and growth under the aegis of an ideal. Not until *the* task becomes *mine* does it come alive in thought and action.

How, then, are such dispositions learned? At the risk of gross oversimplification, I would point to three familiar ways in which we identify ourselves with a quest. First, from dreams, usually engendered by early "exposure", a pure fantasy of oneself doing *that*—wanting to run like Ben Johnson, to sing like Pavarotti. Whether such dreams remain Mitty-esque depends upon opportunity and instruction not to mention such subtle personality factors as having a nose for reality and a tolerance for scrutiny.

Second, dispositions just as frequently emerge from discovery through instruction itself, from the often surprising discovery of personal competencies or potentialities revealed in trying something new. As mentioned, there is an inherent thrill (or positive reinforcement, if you prefer) in realising that one *can do* something well, even at rudimentary stages. Whether one is willing to endure the subsequent pain of instruction depends upon not only the strength of one's personal vision, but also upon the availability of *critical support*.[1] How else could the participants endure the revealing spectacle of Mme. Nilsson's master class? Without something larger than one's ego at stake, the burden of exposure would be unbearable.

Thirdly, and most broadly, I am inclined to say that dispositions, positive or negative, are mostly learnt by example: from the people we admire or loathe; from teachers who drill, explain, and inevitably demonstrate in their own persons what it is to be and to do *that*; from observing with increasing acuity (and independence) the accomplishments of others. The experience becomes self sustaining when at last one learns to learn *unassisted* from close scrutiny of others' achievements. In that way, even a bad performance by a great virtuoso becomes the occasion for critical appreciation and self instruction.

In all this, the imagination sustains critical hindsight and foresight, not so much as a matter of "inspiration", but rather as of *control* within a means-ends continuum linking the necessary skills to the propelling disposition to do well. I hasten to add that as teachers we are not responsible for everything that happens within so complex a nexus of forces. The point bears mentioning as caution against the teacher's *hubris* of taking undue credit or blame for the learner's success or failure. Suffice to recall that learners have their responsibilities too, and that every learner of any age brings innumerable preformed habits and dispositions to the task, some of which, sadly, may be intractable. Fortunately, the old cliché about the Will finding its Way often reverses itself: where a Way can be found, so usually can the Will.

The Basics of Creativity and Critical Thinking

As an offshoot of the "back to basics" movement in recent years, a great deal has been made of creative and critical thinking. An immense literature of uneven quality has grown up around the topics of creativity and critical thinking, enough to justify describing them as "movements" in educational pedagogy and research. Among works of lasting significance in both fields I would mention *inter alia* those of Csikszentmihalyi (1975), Perkins (1981), McPeck (1981), Nickerson (1982), Gardner (1983), Scheffler (1985), and Siegel (1988). Notwithstanding the fierce attention devoted to these topics, certain thoughtless trends about thinking are rife and worth avoiding, especially where the arts are concerned.

A legacy of nineteenth century faculty psychology was "faculty curriculum" supposed to develop certain mental and moral traits: literature and the arts for the sensibilities, logic and mathematics for the intellect, sport and military training for character, and so on. Similar assumptions also riddle the common nonsense about creativity and critical thinking wherein the latter are construed as supervenient mental capacities—kinds of super skill—consisting of specifiable sub-skills. Each, in other words, comes with its own special "bag of tricks". The latter are often assumed to be exhaustive of the super skill; that is, not merely necessary but sufficient. (Cf. McPeck, 1981, p. 8) Hence, learn "synectics" or "lateral thinking" and ye shall be creative! Learn logic, or some variation thereof, and ye shall be a critical thinker! Nobody of course subscribes to these views as just stated, but they lurk in the background as a hidden agendum, as yet another instance of the wistful wish to achieve high ends by fixed means.

Add to this muddle the further too common assumption that creativity and rationality occupy separate mental domains, and the historical circle is nearly complete. Among the adjectives presumably staking out the domain of the Creative: spontaneous, intuitive, subjective, personal, imaginative, inspired, expressive, emotional, associative. A similar, contrasting list circumscribes the domain of the Critical: rational, logical, factual, truthful, disciplined, objective, public, precise, linear, testable, and the like.

And to complete the circle: what subject areas reflect these dichotomous domains? Why, those are the arts and sciences respectively, with the humanities loosely mediating between, leaning now towards "knowledge" (history, philosophy) and now towards "self expression" (poetry, painting, and of course, music). And so one dichotomy engenders another, the one distorting our view of mental processes, the other our views of art, science, and the humanities.

Such a simplistic and misleading scheme alienates even as it misrepresents, leaving us confused as to what art and science are, what as symbolic constructions they do, what the complex relations among them are, and what it takes to do them well. It is a short step from here to labelling the presumed domains of "knowledge" and of "self expression" as "basics" and "frills" respectively. Obviously, this happens time and again in public debates over educational priorities with disastrous and vexing results for art and science instruction alike.

This is not the place to reply to epistemic prejudices except to note that any of the adjectives occurring in the one list above could as easily occur in the other. Certainly Mme. Nilsson's instruction could be described as objective, precise, factual, disciplined, and logical as well as expressive, intuitive, personal, and the like. And by the same token, an unimaginative, uncreative science is a contradiction in terms.

If truth is cheap in science, emotion is more often a means than an end in both art and science. One pursues a problem in physics or philosophy out of felt curiosity that is logically shaped. At the same time, to play "expressively" or, more generally, to express emotion through art is not merely to indulge in depression, joy, or passion. It is, rather, a discipline of the emotions to learn how to use and explore them through the symbolic constructions of art. (See Chapter 3 below) Otherwise, a shout is as good as a symphony.

That brings me to the central point of this discussion; namely, that music education is education of an understanding that ranges from physical dexterity, to emotive discovery, to perceptual insight, to pattern recognition, to associative hunches, to logical argument—in no particular order and in every combination. Moreover, small acts of imagination mediate the many ways of understanding throughout, from running scales to public performances, from merely hearing to learned listening. If not alone in developing and continually calling upon these capacities, music is at the very least a vast and diverse arena for their highest exercise. Such an understanding is not only of music and what it does or means in and of itself, but of what it reveals about ourselves, about our own and other times, and about the many worlds of culture. Becoming educated about music is to create the conditions of music educating us in turn.

Clearly, I am assuming that such understanding, however cultivated by whatever subjects or experiences, is a "good thing", perhaps the best thing that we can expect of an education that is liberal (in the original sense of liberating from ignorance) and humane (also in the original sense of probing our humanity). So what justifies the pursuit of understanding in any of its forms? My all too brief answer is, nothing, or perhaps everything. Or, in Goodman's words, "The point of having leisure time, of a decent moral climate, of prosperity beyond basic need, lies in what these can help make possible. The plays, the music, the mathematical physics, and painting and sculpture do not pose the question 'Why?'; they answer it." (Goodman, 1984, p. 178)

Refrain

Nothing in what I have been saying here runs against the many differences of method, purpose, symbolic construction, sensory modality, or meaning to be found among artistic, humanistic, and scientific disciplines. Rather, my purpose has been to suggest how they serve a common aim of understanding whilst pursuing specifically very different ends-in-view. Neither should I want to leave the impression that any epistemic philosophy will ever summarily say "what it all adds up to", for that would be to destroy the many different ways of understanding a many faceted world. As Isadora Duncan is purported to have said, "If I could say it, I wouldn't bother to dance it". Still, I hope that the foregoing remarks will have shed some light on how the imaginings of music contribute to the growth of understanding, including, perhaps especially, those exact, revealing little imaginings like the "smelling of a flower".

Notes

1 The notion of critical support is crucial for understanding apprenticeship relationships of the kind discussed herein. Yet nowhere to my knowledge is its role in the personal growth of disciplinary values examined. An odd oversight considering the amount of attention that educators have devoted to the so-called problem of "motivation".

References

Mihaly Csikszentmihalyi, *Beyond Boredom and Anxiety* (San Francisco: Jossey Bass, 1975).

John Dewey, *Art as Experience* (New York: Putnam, 1958); first published in 1934.

John Dewey, *Theory of Valuation* (Chicago: University of Chicago Press, 1972); first published in 1939.

Howard Gardner, *Frames of Mind* (New York: Basic Books, 1983).

Nelson Goodman, *Of Mind and Other Matters* (Cambridge: Harvard University Press, 1984).

V. A. Howard, *Artistry: The Work of Artists* (Indianapolis: Hackett, 1982).

V. A. Howard and J. H. Barton, *Thinking on Paper* (New York: William Morrow, 1986).

Frederick Husler and Yvonne Rodd-Marling, *Singing, the Physical Nature of the Vocal Organ* (London: Hutchinson, 1976).

John McPeck, *Critical Thinking and Education* (New York: St. Martin's Press, 1981).

New Yorker Magazine, December 1984, pp. 44-45.

Raymond S. Nickerson, *Notes About Reasoning* (Cambridge: Bolt, Beranek and Newman, 1982).

D. N. Perkins, *The Mind's Best Work* (Cambridge: Harvard University Press, 1981).

Israel Scheffler, *Conditions of Knowledge, An Introduction to Epistemology and Education* (Chicago: Scott, Foresman, 1965); reprinted by the University of Chicago Press, 1986.

Israel Scheffler, *Of Human Potential* (London: Routledge & Kegan Paul, 1985).

Harvey Siegel, *Educating Reason, Rationality, Critical Thinking and Education* (New York: Routledge, Chapman & Hall, 1988).

3

Expression as Hands On Construction

> Poetry is the breath and finer spirit of all knowledge; it is the
> impassioned expression which is in the countenance of all science.
> —Wordsworth

Expression as "Hands Off"

How do artists find expression through art? Commenting in *Art as Experience* on the "nature of spontaneous expression", John Dewey redirects some of William James' remarks on religious experience as follows:

> "What William James wrote about religious experience might well have been written about the antecedents of acts of expression. 'A man's conscious wit and will are aiming at something only dimly and inaccurately imagined . . . and his conscious strainings are letting loose subconscious allies behind the scenes which in their way work toward rearrangement, and the rearrangement toward which all these deeper forces tend is . . . definitely different from what he consciously conceives and determines. It may consequently be actually interfered with (jammed as it were) by his voluntary efforts slanting toward the true direction.' Hence, as he adds, 'When the new centre of energy has been subconsciously incubated so long as to be just ready to burst into flower, 'hands off' is the only word for us; it must burst forth unaided.'" (Dewey, 1934, p. 72)

It is commonplace, not only among philosophers and psychologists, to think of expression in ways suggesting that "subconscious maturation precedes creative production in every line of human endeavour". (Dewey 1934, p. 73) Still, without denying that acts of expression may often *feel* incogitant, Dewey *via* James' words manages to evoke a number of troublesome corollaries of expression as a "hands off" affair.

First is the notion that expression is less a matter of what one *does* than of what one *undergoes*, a subliminal happening, as it were, that eventually overwhelms the paltry results of conscious effort. "The direct effort of 'wit and will'", says Dewey, "of itself never gave birth to anything that is not mechanical." (1934, p. 73) Second is the view that expression is entirely subjective, emotional, as well as passive in its maturation and essentially non-cognitive, i.e., having little to do with "understanding" as such. Third, and following from the preceding, is the idea that expression is not something the artist *controls* and manipulates (for that would be "mechanical") but rather *inspires* or takes in (like a breath of fresh Muse). Finally is the suggestion that the artist is no less a surprised *discoverer* of what he or she has done in a work of art than any other onlooker—rather like being a blind seer of one's own accomplishments—"Oh, look, what I've said!" "See what I've painted!" "Hear what I've sung!" uttered in genuine surprise at the outcome.

Certainly we do often feel ourselves possessed by a task, subjectively immersed in it, propelled by it, surprised by our own achievements, and not only in art. Nevertheless, exclusive stress on the subjective roots of expression yields a portrait of the expressive artist as a mindless media mechanic whose primary goal is to get Mind out of the way of the flow of the Muse. For artists and audiences alike, on this view, finding or understanding expression is not something to be deliberately worked at. Left properly alone, it will work *on* you.

No one who has witnessed serious artists at work, tried to get a feel for their work, or better yet, experienced first hand the rigours of training in virtually any artistic domain can consistently hold to such a view. Each of the aforementioned corollaries of "hands off" expression, I maintain, is a partial truth parading as a whole truth, the kernels of which do yet deserve preservation in a more comprehensive view of expression that reconciles mystery with mastery both in works of art and in the work of artists.

So far I have been deliberately mixing talk of expression by artists and by their works. Now I want to disentangle such talk in an attempt to place expressive process and expressive product in mutual perspective. That is a tall order for a few pages, so I shall need to harken back occasionally to previously published studies of mine examining aspects of expression as a symbolic function of works of art. Those studies drew heavily upon Goodman's notion of expression as metaphoric exemplification within a variety of symbolic systems. (Goodman, 1972, pp. 45-95; Howard, 1971, 1978)

For me then, as for Goodman, expression was viewed from the standpoint of the finished work of art, the product, as something a work of art itself *does*: namely, it exemplifies within a syntactically and semantically dense symbolic system. The basic idea was that a work of art functions symbolically in certain ways to express a range of its metaphoric properties. For reasons of space I shall take much of that work for granted without the details of supporting distinctions and arguments.

Herein I want to consider the other side of the coin: what the *artist* does to produce an expressive effect, broadly speaking, notwithstanding the fact that art works can go on to speak for themselves in ways often outstripping the artist's intentions. I shall argue that performing expressively, finding expression in a work of art, or producing a work that is expressive in some way are all "hands on" constructive activities directing rather than following the rush of feelings.

Expression as Hands Tied

Expression is usually thought to be *of* emotion, and, therefore, to have its deepest origins somewhere in the unconscious. So, to be an expressive performer, to express oneself in an art form, even to grasp the expressive outpourings of other persons through their art requires being "in touch" with those upwellings. And that means getting out of their way, letting them happen, and avoiding obstructions such as "thinking" or doing too much. It's hands off in the sense of hands tied while the emotions work their way upon us.

This notion of expression as passive affection has a long history going back to Plato's description in the *Ion* of the poet as a "light and winged thing, and holy, and never able to compose until he has become inspired, and is beside himself, and reason is no longer within him". (*Ion*, 534 b) The suggestion is that emotional inspiration bypasses reason and under-standing both in its origins and expressive functions. Either as god-given gift or as native talent, the artist's powers of expression appear as nonrational "inspirations" (literally, breathings in) from a mysterious place in the Soul or Universe.

In common practice, passive affection is linked to an arousal theory of expression according to which the artist gets "pumped up" for a performance, or in order to write or to paint expressively *versus* routinely. Again, too much "thinking" is considered an interference, likely to "jam" the subliminal machinery. As a voice teacher of mine used to advise, "Put your heart as well as your head into it, Vernon".

Good advice, so far as it goes. But what is the "it" into which the heart is supposed to go? It is not enough simply to say, "the work" (as end product). Quite clearly, a good deal of technical proficiency, a sense of direction, of particular ends-in-view, estimates of appropriate or inappropriate emphasis are also required. As well, one is required to possess a fair degree of competency (in the sense of thoughtful use) of the symbolic medium through which one seeks expression. These are the means of expression. Otherwise, a shout is as good as a song, a blot on paper as good as a *bon mot*.

All that, I should maintain, is implicit in my teacher's advice to put heart *as well as* head into the effort to sing expressively. She was *not* suggesting that I put all thought aside but rather to attend more *via* my own feelings to the feelings expressed by the work being rehearsed. So already we have a qualification on the original dichotomy of Mind and Muse in the way that skills and expression combine in actual practice.

But who is in the lead, Mind or Muse? The question is misleading in still clinging to the dichotomy. In practice good writers, performers, sculptors, and the like seldom wait passively for inspiration to strike, but go in pursuit of it by prodding, practicing, and producing something "out there"—a result however tentative. I am reminded of a parallel in writing instruction where, "we do not so much send our thoughts in pursuit of words as use words to pursue our thoughts." (Howard and Barton, 1986, p. 24) In effect, *finding* expression or inspiration, on whatever meaning, is more the reward for an effort made than the gift of a secret puppeteer working behind the scenes; that is, artists—productive ones anyway—deliberately seek expression by whatever symbolic means more often than waiting for it, Godot-like, to happen to them and only then to clamp their feelings into symbolic form.

Now if finding expression is more a matter of working than of waiting, more a matter of results achieved than of mysterious origins, what distinguishes those moments of felt fluency and expressiveness from jerky routine and stoppages? In a word, obstacles; usually quite public (if not obvious to anyone) obstacles in the work at hand. (Cf. Howard, 1982, pp. 32-35) By obstacles in the work at hand I refer to problems of execution, as in singing or acting, as well as to problems of construction, as in putting together the elements of a plot line or combining colour and plane in a painting. Too often we attribute blocks to a wrong state of mind, perhaps involving "trying too hard". That may happen, of course; but the attribution to one's state of mind is often hasty. Just as often something more straightforward is responsible: an obstacle in the work itself. Such obstacles are open to public scrutiny by teachers and critics (including self critics) thereby opening opportunities for evaluation and revision. Making such changes is very much a hands on affair, as likely to be Mind over Muse as the reverse, and recognizable more in the expressiveness (or lack of it) in the work one does than in the quantity of emotion felt, whatever its origins.

Expression as Hands Aflutter

The second and third corollaries of hands off expression can be characterized together as "hands aflutter". As described at the outset, that is the view that expression is entirely subjective, emotional, as well as passive in its genesis and essentially incogitant, having little to do with understanding. In *trying* to express something, or oneself, through a work of art, the artist is more the medium than the manipulator of expression; more the sensitive collector of expressive "vibrations" than the deliberate controller of expressive effects. Again, the not so thinly veiled suggestion is that too much "trying", too much "thinking", are bad habits in art.

This is a good spot to underscore the fact that, contrary to popular opinion, expression is not always of emotion; that pictures, for example, can express sounds and physical motions as well as emotions, that music can express colours and spaces as well as feelings. (Goodman, 1972, pp. 85-95; Howard, 1971, p. 274) It is easy to imagine a silent, highly agitated work of dance expressing properties of sound or of physical inertia. Furthermore, as Goodman notes, "A painter or composer does not have to have the emotions he expresses in his work." (Goodman, 1972, p. 47) Neither of course need the dancers in the aforementioned silent, quick moving work prep themselves by shouting while standing stock still. Getting "in the mood" to paint, to compose, or to perform is not necessarily getting into the *same* emotional state as gets expressed in the work; still less so if the expression is of something other than emotion.

Yet the idea persists that getting in the mood is entirely emotional and subjective, however we get there, notwithstanding failure of the simplistic notion of the artist-as-emotional-sluice. No doubt, "warming up" is a vital part of preparation sometimes, a flexing of technical skills such as running scales, stretching, or making corrections in the previous evening's manuscript. Clearly more deliberate and cognitive than merely standing aside hands aflutter, such preparations nevertheless do aim at putting oneself in a state of "receptivity"; receptivity now not only to emotions (if we must allow for nonemotional expression) but to the metaphoric *feel* of sounds, spaces, colours, or whatever one is trying to express. But then, it will be argued, after working ourselves up "technically", we can let go of routine control in order to let the powers of expression take over.

I concede that flat calm is hardly the best mood to walk on stage and that emotions have many roles to play in "getting set". For instance, is this something you want to do? Feel confident to do? Are you overanxious? Still, the idea of letting go at the top, as it were, misleads in suggesting that judgement applies only to *where* to deploy routine skills but drops out when expressive spontaneity takes over. Elsewhere I have argued at length that critical judgement (control) is crucial not only to the acquisition and deployment of technical facilities in art, but at the highest levels of artistry be it in performance or the creation of new works. (Howard, 1982, pp. 181-185)

Even—perhaps especially—when technical facilities are safely tucked away in physical or mental memory, judgement and choice come to the fore in the form of decisions of taste and of style. Far from occupying separate compartments, expression in art is a form of control in which emotion and much more takes shape in what is properly called the *work* of art. Such a view of expression as controlled work conflicts head on, however, with the notion of expression in performance or elsewhere in art as passive arousal unfiltered by effort and understanding.

While it is crucial to be poised, focussed, receptive, or otherwise "in the mood" to produce an expressive effect in art, such receptivity is a deliberate funneling of feeling in planned ways and directions. One is reminded of Kathleen Ferrier's dramatic last recording with Bruno Walter of Mahler's *Das Lied von Der Erde* on the very afternoon she received the diagnosis of her fatal illness. Instead of sitting down and weeping into her hands, she wept into—one might better say through—Mahler's songs. In effect, she *made* something artistic out of her feelings very much in a "hands on" manner.

Expression as Hands in the Air

If expression is construed as more a happening than a making, then it is bound to come as a complete surprise, something of a "hands in the air" discovery after the fact. One weaves away like Odysseus' Penelope, and lo, an effect is born much to one's own surprise as to anyone else's. "If artists only find out what their emotions are in the course of finding out how to express them, they cannot begin the work of expression by deciding what emotion to express." So said Collingwood in the *Principles of Art* (1938, p. 117), the most sustained effort in print to avoid a "fabrication" theory of art. The trouble with this view of expression we-know-not-what-nor-whence-nor-whither is that it robs the artist of all control by foresight (not to be confounded with foreknowledge or prediction). (Cf. Howard, 1982, pp. 117-120)

No doubt artists do sometimes clarify or discover their emotions in the act of expressing them; that is not at issue. What I question (aside from the already noted restriction of expression to emotion) is the stronger claim that artists *only* discover their emotions—or anything else expressible—by actually expressing them. For one thing, it seems perfectly comprehensible that one can know in advance *what* one wants to express, if only vaguely, without being able to do so, or to do so effectively; but let us go to cases to see exactly what gets discovered in the attempt.

Recall again the master class in singing conducted by Mme. Birget Nilsson, especially Mr. Barth's predicament. "Mr. Barth was invited back to the final class. He sang 'Per me giunto', from Verdi's *Don Carlos*. Mme. Nilsson soon had Mr. Barth concentrating on the aria's final phrase, *'morrá per te'*, which contains all the passion of a man telling his best friend that he's about to die for him. 'I don't think I would dare to put so much strength on *'morrá'*, Mme. Nilsson warned. 'Start soft. When you think the note is in place, *then* you can open up.'

"Mr. Barth tried it. On the *'morrá'*, his voice wobbled and cracked. He stopped, frowning.

"'I knew that was coming', Mme. Nilsson said, laughing. 'There was too much tension here'—in the larynx. 'Try it again, softer. Maybe we are lucky, maybe not.'

"The accompanist gave Mr. Barth his note, he took a breath, and what came out this time was almost a new voice—open, firm, and brilliant." (New Yorker, 1984)

Now what did Mr. Barth discover? One might just reply, "How much he could *do!*"—a hands on statement if ever there was one, but let's look closer at the situation. Up to the point of his breakthrough he was unable to properly express the emotional force of the phrase *"morrá per te"*. Did he know what that expressive import was? One can only assume yes, if he studied the text; and there is virtually no chance he'd be allowed on stage with Mme. Nilsson if he hadn't. So again, what did he discover?

Clearly, Mr. Barth had a good idea of what he was aiming for expressively; was technically well prepared to achieve his aim; but failed because of an obstacle. What he discovered—more likely, rediscovered, for a man of his level of competency—was the *means* of expression: a technical manoeuvre that enabled him to get the best out of himself. More than that, he discovered not only a *way* but how *well* he could express the phrase in question; which is to include, among other things, his own personal colouration of the phrase. He made it his own, so to speak. That is indeed a gratifying discovery, but it hardly amounts to a game of artistic blind man's bluff with himself. Less driven by an inspiration than an aspiration, Mr. Barth might well have said to himself, "My word, look what I can do if I only *concentrate*."

The point is balance: if finding the right expression is sometimes accidental, discovery of the sort described above is a product of strenuous effort, not of passive receptivity or accident. However "pumped up" Mr. Barth might have been, he would never have discovered his expressive potential for that single phrase out of *Don Carlos* had he set aside his critical judgement and foresight, not to mention hindsight, of his failure.

The moral of this twice-told story is that discoveries of expressive potential, as of much else in life, are seldom mere "happenings"—accidents—even if some are, but rather the results of directed, discipline effort. We try, we fail, we try again, and sometimes we succeed. Even more painful, thoughtful, exhilarating odysseys of expressive discovery than Mr. Barth's are commonplace among artists. It is a distortion of the tough work they do to reduce it all to the level of "surprise, surprise!"

Expression as Hands On

I began by speaking of expression as sometimes passive, sometimes subjective, sometimes uncontrolled, sometimes surprising, and ended with a story of personal discovery in a public forum. My negative aim was to head off those who would substitute the word 'always' for the word 'sometimes' in the preceding sentence. My positive aim was to sketch a portrait of the quest for expression showing it to be as discerning as it is feeling—a matter of making and, therefore, for the most part a "hands on" constructive affair. To quote Goodman, "Emotion in aesthetic experience is a means of discerning what properties a work of art has and expresses." (Goodman, 1972, p. 248) And that applies as much to what we try to do as to what we finally achieve or appreciate in the work of others.

References

R. G. Collingwood, *The Principles of Art* (London: Oxford University Press, 1967); first published in 1938.

John Dewey, *Art as Experience* (New York: Putnam, 1958); first published in 1934.

Nelson Goodman, *Languages of Art, An Approach to a Theory of Symbols* (Indianapolis: Hackett, 1972).

V. A. Howard, "On Musical Expression", *The British Journal of Aesthetics*, vol. 11 (1971), pp.

V. A. Howard, "Music and Constant Comment", *Erkenntnis*, vol. 12 (1978), pp.

V. A Howard, *Artistry, the Work of Artists* (Indianapolis: Hackett, 1982).

V. A. Howard, and J. H. Barton, *Thinking on Paper* (New York: William Morrow, 1986).

Alfredo Kraus, Remarks made on CBC Radio, 29 June 1985, *Romeo and Juliet*, Dallas Opera Company.

New Yorker Magazine, December 1984, pp. 44-45.

Israel Scheffler, "In Praise of the Cognitive Emotions", in *Inquiries: Philosophical Studies of Language, Science, and Learning* (Indianapolis: Hackett, 1986).

4

One Image is Worth a Thousand Words

Such Stuff as Dreams are Made on

Earlier I spoke of *heuristic imagination* as a "mind set" or selective predilection to specific patterns of thought, action, and perception. The phenomena in question range from "mental rehearsal" and habit formation to metaphoric imagery of the kind employed by Mme. Nilsson above to aspect perception as with Neker cubes or detecting unobvious features of music. Beyond imagery in action and perception are the concoctions of pure fancy: fictional characters and events, unicorns and centaurs.

Straightaway we need to distinguish imagining in the sense of *imaging* or image making from imagining in the sense of *supposing* with or without images. The former is my main concern herein. The latter, supposition, can be quite independent of image making as, for example, when we entertain contrafactual claims such as, "Suppose the world were flat . . . " or "Suppose that a < b".

Now the usual approach to mental imagery is to ask what and where in the world are mental images? Neural firings in the head? Pictures in the mind? But do we really expect the neurologists to discover different Pickwick and Quixote synapses or tiny portraits in a mental gallery? The common sense question leads us into uncommon nonsense. We might do better to ask, what does it *mean* to see, feel, touch, hear, smell, or act, all, as we say in one inclusive metaphor, "in the mind"? Then, depending upon what we mean by such phrases as "seeing in the mind's eye", we should be in better position to broach questions about the existence and nature of mental images.

A good deal rides on the question of the nature of mental images for both cognitive scientists and philosophers. (Cf. Schwartz, 1980; Gardner, 1983, Ch. 11) One problem often noted is that what goes on in the mind's eye, ear, nose, or throat cannot be seen, heard, smelt, nor tasted. A visual mental image of my own face, for instance, occupies no space, cannot be seen by my own eyes, is made of no material pigments, and is not literally drawn (even if, as I am now doing, I imagine myself drawing a self likeness). Nor do I actually smell my own olfactory image of the aroma of last evening's onion soup. (See Goodman, 1988, p. 84) Such shadow entities, if entities at all, seem less facts than figments of imagination. (Cf. Gardner, 1983, p. 323ff)

A hard nosed skeptic might say that an imperceptible, totally insubstantial, unlocatable image is more like a message without a medium than any material image on canvas or film; more likely nothing rather than something. Vivid experience seems to give way under scrutiny to a vacuous concept. At the very least, it is a serious question what sense, if any, can be made of claims to experience things, to perceive them, exclusively "in the mind" whether or not one ever perceived them in the world.

Hume's famous answer to the aforementioned question is that the images of fancy are like ordinary perceptions only fainter, lacking the "vivacity or solidity or firmness or steadiness" that engenders belief. (Hume, 1888, p. 628) In other words, mental imagery in any modality is a kind of weak perceiving in the head. If so, then a difference of veracity—between what does or does not engender belief—reduces to a difference of vivacity with obvious troublesome consequences for artists or anyone, for that matter, of vivid imagination. Mental imagery, particularly fictional and metaphoric varieties, cannot be likened to sensory phantasms or after images, say, of a brightly lit window when we close our eyes. Mme. Nilsson, for example, in her voice lesson recounted earlier did not instruct

Mr. Barth first to stare fixedly at a spotlit flower in her hand and then to shut his eyes and sing!

Ryle's equally famous reply to Hume is that imagining is not perceiving at all, still less weakly in the head. "Picturing" in the mind's eye is nothing like drawing or perceiving a likeness on paper or canvas for all the reasons aforementioned. "Imagining", he says, "is not having shadowy pictures before some shadow-organ called the 'mind's eye'; but having paper pictures before the eyes in one's face is a further stimulus to imagining". (Ryle, 1949, p. 254) Rylc is not of course denying that we have mental images, whatever they are, only that they are like real pictures and perceptions. "We do picture or visualize faces and mountains . . . but picturing a face or mountain is not having before us a picture of a face or mountain . . . " (pp. 254-255)

This may sound like double talk, but the thrust of Ryle's denial that imagining is inwardly perceiving the mental analogues of physical pictures, sounds, and the like, is to forestall the quantifiable existence of mental images taken separately from their real or fictional referents—something we *can* do with physical pictures—like so many portraits of a separately identified sitter.

When, for instance, I describe my image of a face, it is features of the face that I describe, not features of my mental image. Even should it be an image of Charles II's face based upon portraits, still it is features of his face as physically portrayed that I describe and not details of my private, inner portrait. Or, to put it another way, it is the accuracy of the image that concerns us in this case. [1]

Assume I now have in mind an image of Charles II's face: what sense is there in asking *its* size and colouration separately from *his* size and colouration or that of his physical portraits? The futility of the question marks the failure of any attempt to introspect the nature of mental images apart from their contents and what we do when we imagine. (Cf. Mary Warnock on Satre, 1978, pp. 161-166) Incidentally, this line of argument seems quite consistent with Kosslyn's ingenious experiments on the scanning of mental maps. (Kosslyn, et al. 1978, 1983) There too the focus is on what subjects can or cannot do with mental images, not what they are.

Other writers, however, take the argument one step further in claiming that there are no facts based upon observable properties of mental images as such to be known that would enable us to say in any literal way what and where they are. Roger Scruton, for one, says, "Mere 'observation' of our images will tell us nothing about them: the only facts about images are facts about the third person case . . . If we wish to know what an image is, we must ask, 'What is it about another that enables us to say of him that he has images?'" (Scruton, 1974, p. 74) In a similar vein, Mary Warnock remarks that "the image cannot be treated as an independent object which can be examined on its own, even though the word for it must occur in our accounts of imagining. We may need the noun; but to understand it we have to understand the verb." (Warnock, 1978, p. 172)

On the face of it, Scruton's position seems incompatible with recent experimental work on image manipulation in allowing only third person access to facts about them; but that may be an inhospitable interpretation. Rather, I take him to be saying that having images and doing something with them in ways publicly demonstrable is quite different from trying to introspect their inherent nature or physical causes. Still, from Kosslyn's standpoint Scruton overstates his case in saying that there are *no* facts about images to be gleaned from introspection. Without prejudice to their entity-hood, we can at least know *that* and *when* we experience images. And if Kosslyn is right, we can in fact do all sorts of things with them, interpreting and exploring them with varying degrees of accuracy and speed. (Kosslyn, 1978) To that extent, Warnock seems closer to the mark in suggesting that the verb is the key to the noun.

Both Scruton and Warnock skirt the question *whether* images exist while presupposing their phenomenal reality. Yet the questions whether they are—whether we need to postulate them as entities—and when they are, are prior to what they are as entities, what causes them, or how we interpret them; but allow me to defer the ontological issue for the moment.

So what might we say thus far about mental imagery in the growth of performance skills? Something like this: if we are to understand the role of heuristic imagination—the role of imagery in controlling skilled performances—it is not a question of what images *are* in themselves but of what they *do*, how they may function to control (assuming their existence). And notwithstanding the privacy and physical mystery of images, their functions may yet turn out to be surprisingly public—hardly less intersubjective than reports of pains or emotions and other observable effects no less detectable.

Consider, for example, that my experience of toothache is not sharable; the pain is all mine. Yet the facts that I have a cavity, am grimacing and complaining, made an appointment to see the dentist, are observable. Barring deception (and there are ways of checking up on that), the latter add up to strong circumstantial evidence of toothache especially for anyone who has had one himself. Even for someone who never had a toothache, pain is no stranger and the evidence, if a little vaguer, no less convincing. I am suggesting that our knowledge of other people's images is similar, namely, circumstantial and intersubjective; whereas, there is nothing circumstantial or evidential in *having* my own pains or images. No introduction is required.

Image, Reference, Belief

What I just said about "having" images amounts to postulating their existence, in some sense, as entities. That is, in talking pedagogically about what images can *do*, and in making other references to images, I casually presuppose their existence. Yet I would suggest that much of our image talk can be replaced by talk about abilities, tests, standards, and performances. I further suggest that, as an analytic exercise, replacement locutions help to clarify what, besides private mental events, image talk is about in the world of public events. This and the following sections explore how far one can carry the replacement strategy and whether it can be carried through without remainder. If it is possible to replace all references to images by references to something else *without a surplus*, then we should be relieved of any commitment to images as entities. Mental image talk would then turn out to be a kind of picturesque shorthand for talk about other things like abilities and tests. I shall argue that complete elimination of reference to mental images is a questionable undertaking, especially in the pedagogical realm, and maybe in cognitive science as well.

Two common types of heuristic imagination recurrent in these pages are literal and metaphoric imagery. Both depend upon our ability to interpret mental images symbolically. (Cf. Schwartz, 1980, pp. 286 and 289) Literal imagery is imagining X as it is, was, or might be (e.g., Russell Square in the Spring; the sound of Bjoerling's voice; a shape one wishes to draw). Metaphoric imagery is imagining X as something else Y (Churchill as a bulldog; DNA as a double helix; the voice as placed "forward" in the face). Both varieties, it might be argued, while not *depicting* X in shadow pictures observed by the mind's eye, are ways of *representing* X to ourselves. That is the position Warnock takes: "The images we form are necessarily incomplete, but they are ways of representing for ourselves some of the features of the object of our thought, those features which will identify what we are thinking of . . . "—by which she means that, "The image *is* our attempt to reach the nonexistent or absent object in our thoughts as we concentrate on this or that aspect of it, its visible appearance, its sound, its smell." (Warnock, 1978, p. 173)

So instead of thing-like images we have imaginal ways of representing things to ourselves. In other words, the burden of meaning shifts from the noun to the verb *via* representation; from what, if anything, is "in" the mind to how imagining works. The difficulty here is that representation, whatever else it may be, is a form of reference. (Goodman, 1972, pp. 42-43) One thing represents another transitively; but in the cases before us reference by what to what? We seem no further ahead with a view that allows a dyadic relation between "ways of representing" and fictional beings like Pickwick than with image-entities-we-know-not-what.

To avoid such difficulties, a reinterpretation of reference is required to explain how we interpret mental images. One manoeuvre, suggested by Goodman's treatment of fictional pictures and narratives, is to construe "image of X" or "thoughts of X" as one-place rather than two-place predicates; as referring to the *kinds* of images and thoughts we are having: sound-images or Pickwick-thoughts rather than images or thoughts denoting the voice and appearance of a nonexistent Pickwick.

In talking about mental images, unlike physical images, there are *two* questions of existence: first, whether the image exists; and second, whether the putative object of the image exists. The ambiguity is in the prepositions "of" and "about" in *saying* what our thoughts (including imagery) are about. On the two-place construction we are committed to saying what our thoughts taken separately refer to or denote. On the one-place construction what they are about is what they are; the mental image simply *is*, rather than refers to, what it means. This eliminates reference to nonexistent beings while allowing us to entertain in thought and fancy anything we like.

So in describing what our imaginings are "of" or "about", we may only be describing their phenomenal character rather than anything, if anything, to which they separately refer; still less are we alluding to what mental stuff they are made of. This yields at least the following possibilities: we can imagine X as it is, or as we wish X to be, or X as something else Y, or merely entertain an X-image or X as Y-image with or without reference to anything "real"; though, obviously, in *describing* our imaginings we refer to all these possibilities, including the reality in experience of the image itself.

In all but the first case (imagining X as it is), imagining (in the sense of imaging) X as Y and so forth, does not entail a belief that X *is* Y or that anything corresponding to X actually exists. Consequently, imagination does not entail belief even if we do sometimes "believe in" what we imagine—in the sense, say, of trying to bring it about by an effort. The range of exceptions where belief and imagination contingently meet is enlarged, however, if we allow that some cases of imagining X as Y metaphorically (e.g., Churchill as a bulldog) do imply the belief that X is metaphorically Y; that is, when the metaphoric image is referred to a real person or thing.

But how can such reference be accomplished? Was not the whole point of substituting Churchill-images for images of Churchill to avoid commitment to reference in our talk about mental imagery? The answer is yes, by mental images to unreal things, but not to the extent of preventing reference by mental images to real things as, for instance, when I correctly or incorrectly imagine the opening bars of the *Goldberg Variations*. This supposes that mental images, as much as physical ones, can be used symbolically; and here I agree with Robert Schwartz when he says, "In focussing on the way images serve to represent, I am proposing to treat imagery as a kind of symbolisation. All I mean by the claim that images have symbolic functions is that they may bear semantic-type relations to things; they can play a role in describing, depicting, or representing objects, relationships, or 'states of affairs'. This is not the only function of imagery, but it is a prominent one." (1980, p. 186)

This is the point missed by Warnock in her "ways of representing", namely, that representation is a symbolic use of imagery requiring interpretation in one or other symbolic system. (Cf. Goodman, 1972, pp. 42-43) For instance, a visual mental image of two adjacent ovals, 'OO', may be two zeroes, two letter O's, or Little Orphan Annie's eyes depending upon whether the interpretation is in a numerical, linguistic, or pictorial system. This underscores two important points about mental images as symbols: first, that visual images are not always "pictorial" in function, as is commonly assumed; and second, that different symbolic systems may function within the same sensory modality as in the example above. From that it follows that "there is no unique way by which visual imagery phenomena symbolize." (See Schwartz, 1980, pp. 287-288 and 293) The same holds true of symbolisation in any of the other image modalities of sound, touch, or taste with the result that the number and types of symbol systems involved in the interpretation of mental images exhibits the same variety to be found elsewhere in cognition.

To sum up these technicalities thus far: imagination as a species of thought, and mental imagery in particular, can literally or metaphorically reflect our beliefs about things real or fictional in many symbolic ways notwithstanding the *general* disconnection of imagination from belief and reference.

So far, the replacement strategy for eliminating reference to image-entities has fared rather poorly. Indeed, with mental images now functioning symbolically, it is difficult to see what advantages such a strategy could have. But there are some, and I turn now to more serious forays in that direction: first, a limited attempt of my own and then a more comprehensive effort of Goodman's (1988).

From Image to Action

Suppose a singer in training says, "I've got it! I know now exactly the sound I want to make. I can hear it in my mind." Or consider the composer who claims to "hear in my mind the music I want to create"; the choreographer who can "see and feel the movements just thinking about them". Similarly, a practiced musician can often "hear" the music he or she is silently reading for the first time. What is such talk about? Whatever is going on *in mens*, the tests *in re* for such enlightenment are public demonstrations, not introspected dawnings. Anyone who says such things is expected to be able to make the sound, produce the piece, perform the music.

This suggests a way of replacing talk about imagery and imagination directing performance—in effect, accommodating the control factor by "translating" such talk into statements about how well or badly one performs. Generally, to make such claims as those above is to say that one can respond with a degree of accuracy to certain questions, tests, or stimuli. Hence, the fidelity of the image reduces to facility of response or other behavioural function as measured by public standards. We are now talking about demonstrable abilities and skills.

So, for instance, my saying that I have a clear image or "idea" in mind of the sound I want to produce may be taken as a fanciful, picturesque way of saying that I thereby constitute myself an instrument that says "yes" to some adjustments and "no" to others—that I set myself to "go off" at some point, to do certain things in certain ways. One could think of this as the focussing phase of a kind of ideo-motor action wherein I take private measure of the action to come. I as well as others may take the measure of the action as completed; that much is fully public.

Conversely, I as instrument also have the capacity to respond to tests as to whether the mental images or other advice given to me by others—colleagues, coaches, teachers—are clear or useful.

As a learner I am in a privileged position to complain about confusing or misleading advice. Had Mme. Nilsson instructed Mr. Barth in his vocal distress to imagine that he was a cricket while projecting his voice from his kneecaps, there is nothing short of slapstick and a squeak that he could have done to conform to such vaudevillean advice.

Seen from this angle, heuristic imagery may fail like any other figure of speech and for the same reasons: through being misconceived, misdirected, mistimed, or simply misunderstood. Beyond the learner's queries and responses to imagery, the teacher's repertoire of illustrations and demonstrations offers the best indication of their meanings for action, and simultaneously, the best defense against misinterpretation, plain nonsense, or deliberate quackery. Like the open lesson recounted in Chapters 2 and 3, all this is quite public business the success or failure of which depends as much on action as on introspection of imagery. In the final result, the mind's jumble takes a back seat to what does or does not get done.

The theoretical advantage of construing such imagery as fanciful descriptions of one's adjustment as an instrument is to project the image forward, as it were, as a *standard* by which to measure one's reactions to particular stimuli before and after responding. Imagining X, or X as Y, just *is* the function of setting the standard, while doing X "with imagination" is the function of responding to the standard—the effort made to approximate to the advice set forth in the imagery. We now get a better idea of what imagery does in learning.

The practical advantage of sometimes construing imagery talk as referring to standards and performances is that it gives us the desired third-person purchase on the meaning and value of such talk in the areas of "know-how" and disciplined action. We get a better idea of what we do in using and responding to imagery.

Notice, however, that in explicating what image talk is about, behaviourally and evaluatively, in instructional contexts, that I have not entirely eliminated reference to imagery. I am not treating them as *entia non grata*, as "defective nouns", in Quine's words, like sakes and behalves in the prepositional phrases, "For the sake of . . . ", "On the behalf of . . . " (Quine, 1960, p. 244)

Sakes and behalves can be paraphrased away, but not so mental images in teaching and learning.

The notion of images as entities is embedded in practice. Talking about what images do and of what we do in response to them presupposes that they exist. So long as reference is made to "it" (the image), one is committed to images as entities. One instructs the student to "hear the sound mentally", "rehearse the phrase in your mind", "keep the flower smelling image in mind as you sing", etc. The student is expected to do exactly that, to keep "it" in mind, and to do even more in performance as described above. The point is that in cases of imagery controlling action, in mental rehearsal, and in the teaching and coaching of performance skills, *total* replacement of image talk is impractical, uneconomical. One needs to keep imagery in the logically referential place. Otherwise, the instructions would become unwieldy and incomprehensible. For example, directing a novice singer to inspan the nasal pharynx is far less efficient than suggesting that he or she imagine a deep yawn while producing the tone. Furthermore, even as the replacement idiom explicates the imagery in terms of what one can or cannot do, so conversely, the imagery is often a condition for doing it, as in the example just cited.

Tough Talk About Mental Images

Goodman's latest word on imagery is akin to the approach taken herein and springs from a common interest in the theory of symbols. (Goodman, 1988) However, Goodman focusses primarily on the ontic status of mental imagery in cognitive science, whereas I am more concerned with the governing role of imagery in disciplined action and learning generally. Yet, the same *theoretical* issues arise whether imagery is viewed from a psychological or a pedagogical perspective. Questions of what and where in the world are they, and what it means to have or to act on imagery are inescapable. Still, tolerances for such "unobservables" differ as do degrees of reliance upon them at different levels of explaining and directing learning, as we have seen.

Goodman's strategy for coping with the embarrassing elusiveness of mental imagery for cognitive science is to replace all talk about "having" images or "picturing in the mind" with statements about image-descriptions and depictions. This means, for example, that my having in mind a picture of Capri is to be "construed in terms of my ability to describe or picture or sort out descriptions or pictures of the image—though any descriptions or pictures I produce or encounter will not be *of* the image but rather image descriptions and image pictures." (Goodman, 1988, p. 87; italics his)

This parallels the replacement strategy of the previous section except that (1) it amounts to full replacement of the idiom of mental imagery by the idiom of skills and image-descriptions; and (2) it eliminates any ontic commitment to mental images by assimilating mental image talk to talk about fictional entities. Mental images themselves are put in the same category as Pickwick as being describable without supposing their existence.

Hence, on Goodman's view, "We no longer need go hunting for images any more than we need to go hunting for centaurs. Yet if a centaur happens to pass by some day we can easily accommodate to that without much trouble, though if a mental image liberated itself and fell on the desk before me, I doubt if I could recognize it as such. What really matters is that we are not committed to there being any centaurs or images; but neither are we committed to there being none." (Goodman, 1988, p. 90; Cf. also Dennett, 1978, pp. 174-180)

If this sounds a little like having one's cake-image and deleting it too, the reason is that with fictional entities, considerable independent evidence points to their nonexistence; whereas with mental images, the weight of intersubjective experience points in the opposite direction.

Goodman himself says as much at the beginning of his paper. ". . . we talk quite confidently of the mental images we have, of their clarity or vagueness, of details present or missing, of manipulating and experimenting on such images. We can describe them, picture them, compare them with other images or with their objects. We know what it is to succeed or fail in trying to conjure up an image, and can compare our own experience of images with that of other people. Indeed, discourse about images is in this sense hardly less intersubjective than discourse about objects." (Goodman, 1988, p. 84)

Against this intersubjective, experiential reality of mental imagery—their "episodic" nature, as it were—stand all the considerations aforementioned: their utter privacy and total lack of material or observational access. That is what puts them beyond the empirical pale. Far better, then, it would seem, to concentrate on what is publicly accessible, observable, estimable; namely, image descriptions, depictions, and the exercise of "certain skills—a matter of producing, judging, revising certain *material* pictures and descriptions." (Goodman, 1988, p. 90; italics mine)

The crucial question here is whether the replacement strategy can be carried through without a surplus; whether mental images can be defined or paraphrased away like sakes and behalves. Goodman stops short of that when he says, ". . . we are not committed to there being any centaurs or images; but neither are we committed to there being none." (1988, p. 90) His neutrality here is necessary for, ". . . the treatment of image-talk I have been suggesting", he says, "is not a quick and easy excision of some pseudoentities; it does not amount to translation by routine application of a simple formula. Indeed, although I have spoken loosely of it as translation, it is hardly that; for translation of nonsense would presumably still be nonsense. Rather, what goes on is replacement of statements ostensibly about images by statements about objects and events." (1988, p. 89)

In short, Goodman advocates "replacement" of image talk in cognitive science wherever possible but not without a surplus of (presumably scientific) "nonsense". That is why he leaves it open that there *may* be images after all. As a recommendation, his replacement manoeuvre is intended to make it easier for cognitive scientists to carry on their experimental work with a smaller ontological base. In other words, he thinks cognitive science doesn't *need* images-as-entities in its quest to explain the phenomena of mental imagery.

The strategy is an ingenious one, and goes far towards clarifying the symbolic skills and other abilities comprising the observable phenomena alluded to in mental image talk; but as Goodman is well aware, it remains a contingent matter whether even psychologists can entirely dispense with images as entities. Time and experiment will tell.

So, in lieu of complete, definitional replacement of statements about mental images by statements that do not refer to them, it comes down to a question of need. I am skeptical whether even psychology can do without the surplus of image entities in explaining some of the learning phenomena described in these pages. And for the reasons aforementioned (see pp. 48-49 above), I am far less convinced of the plausibility of full elimination in theory or practice of mental image talk from the domains of teaching and learning.[2] At the very least, the burden of proof is to show otherwise; that mental image talk is eliminable, without loss of economy or explanatory power, from the language of learning and instruction along with the stronger commitment to images as entities that entails.

Second Thoughts On Having Mental Images

While I agree that "our image-talk raw and unprocessed is a terrible tangle" and that talk of imagery "in the mind" is literal nonsense and "taken metaphorically needs careful interpretation" (Goodman, 1988, pp. 89 and 91), nonetheless, there may be a way of talking about "having" mental images that alleviates some of these difficulties.

What we seek is a way of characterizing the "possession" of mental images in somewhat less thing-like language—not to the exclusion of image entities but in a way that focusses upon the differences between those times when we have them and when we don't.

Just as there is usually a clear difference between a person who is conscious and one who is not (barring sham unconsciousness), so also, there is a difference between those times when one can mentally hear a tune, and when one cannot. Such states as being conscious or having a certain image in mind are variously manifest to ourselves and to others: in what we say, how we behave, respond to instruction, and so on. And clearly, when I mentally "hear" a tune, e.g., an irritating repeating melody, something quite different is happening from when I don't hear it.

What does it mean to "have" such experiences? Construed as a one-place rather than two-place predicate, "having an image" becomes a literal property ascription applicable to a person and describing a certain state of that person. That is, to say "Jones is having an image of X" is equivalent to "Jones-is-X-imaging" predicated of Jones, the person, as a property rather than a relation. And for every other image Jones has, there is another predicate as needed to describe all those image states: Q-imaging, R-imaging, and so on. Each image-as-entity is thus incorporated into yet another state of Jones that is subject to verification in all the usual ways. This strategy leaves open the question of images as entities while also allowing us to use Goodman's image descriptions and other tests to verify Jones' state.

On the other hand, that is not enough for teaching and learning. As already noted, some teaching requires talking directly about images as if they existed. One may ask the student to hold an image in mind, to compare or alter it, as if it were a quantifiable entity. In that case, such direct reference to mental images may be construed as metaphorical discourse, as a roundabout way of talking about states of Jones. Which is to say, the interpretive, pedagogical statements, with all their ontic commitment, are so many metaphorical replacements for the literal, one-place property ascription, "X-imaging" to Jones. In this way, we can cash out mental image talk either in the direction of the one-place, literal predicate, "having an image" or in the direction of Goodman's symbolic capacities and other kinds of skills and tests.

All this leaves open the real existence of images *in mens* while providing for every means of their verification and testing *in re*, not to mention leaving us free to talk about them as vividly as we like, or need to.

Getting Physical About Imagery

One hesitates to raise the vexing issue of possible physical explanations of mental imagery. How can physiology explain something that is at best metaphorically described on my account or entirely fictional on Goodman's?

With characteristic conciseness, Goodman outlines his view as follows. "When a physiologist says in effect that a certain image consists of a certain pattern of firings of cells in the cerebral cortex, he is reporting on painstaking scientific investigation. But how has he validated this formulation? Surely, by checking it not against pictures he finds and examines in the brain but against verbal reports and other behaviour of the subject. Such a physiological account and the sort of philosophical account I have outlined are complementaries. Putting them together we get, with some ellipsis, something roughly like this: when firings of the required kind occur in certain cells, the subject can to some extent produce, sort out, criticize, revise, descriptions or pictures of a horse. The 'image' and the 'picture in the mind' have vanished; mythical inventions have been beneficially excised." (Goodman, 1988, p. 91)

From the standpoint of teaching and learning, there is something distinctly unsatisfactory about this account, and I shall try to say in the simplest possible terms what it is.

First, in fairness to Goodman, he is more concerned to stake out a viable third-person (i.e., scientific) perspective on mental imagery than to save the sanctity of the first-person perspective as I am trying to do. So we may actually not be in conflict here. Still, from the latter viewpoint, images *do* have a vital if puzzling presence in consciousness quite independent of their physical causes or tests of their kinds and accuracy. They at least exist in mental time if not in any mental space as episodic ripples in the stream of consciousness—with only such overflowing metaphors to capture the fact. So what may be beneficially excised from scientific theory is not so easily excised from experience. And that is as it should be; for it is not the purpose of any scientific explanation, or practical use of imagery to guide action, for that matter, to *reproduce* the experience of images. It is enough that we can have them, by any account, to be able to use them.

Democracy and Imagination

In choosing to focus on what I call "heuristic imagination"—all those useful little imaginings that can facilitate learning—I am, as said earlier, purposely ignoring much that travels under the label of 'imagination'. Even so, I am not at all suggesting that everything we do "with imagination" is a tandem or two-tiered performance of imagining now and acting later. (See Chapter 2, p. 13 above)   As one friendly to such thinking-in-action notions as "thinking with your hands", "thinking on paper" (Howard and Barton, 1986), and "thinking in performance", I should not want to underrate those times when it is better to think with one's feet instead of one's head. Rather, my concern here and in the two preceding chapters has been to do theoretical justice to that large minority of cases where imagery, so-called mental rehearsal, and metaphoric guidance are ingredient to learning and the personal growth of standards of performance.

Precisely because I place so much emphasis upon the various roles of imagination in learning from humble finger drills to dress rehearsals, it has been suggested to me that I have "democratized" imagination by removing it from its aesthetic throne and putting it to work in mundane circumstances. I accept that description inasmuch as imagination has been traditionally conceived as either a mysterious gift of the Muse or as the frosting on a layer-cake of drudgerously (and sometimes mindlessly) acquired skills. With so many tough jobs to do, imagination at honest toil gains in learning power what it loses in hollow status at leisure.

Notes

1   The same holds true of mental images of fictional beings like Pickwick whose features are separately depicted and described in the illustrated Dickens. I should be wrong, for instance, were I to have an image of Pickwick that was closer to the actor David Niven than to Leo McKern.

2   And that is notwithstanding the usefulness of occasional replacement of the imagery idiom along the lines of the previous Section 2 aimed at elucidating the complex relations among images, standards, and performances.

References

D. C. Dennett, *Content and Consciousness* (London: Routledge & Kegan Paul, 1969).

D. C. Dennett, *Brainstorms* (Cambridge: Bradford/MIT Press, 1978).

N. F. Dixon, *Subliminal Perception, The Nature of a Controversy* (London: McGraw-Hill, 1971).

Howard Gardner, *The Mind's New Science* (New York: Basic Books, 1983).

·Nelson Goodman, *Languages of Art, An Approach to a General Theory of Symbols* (Indianapolis: Hackett, 1972).

Nelson Goodman, "On Thoughts Without Words", in *Of Mind and Other Matters* (Cambridge: Harvard University Press, 1984).

Nelson Goodman and Catherine Z. Elgin, "Sights Unseen", in *Reconceptions in Philosophy and Other Arts and Sciences* (Indianapolis: Hackett, 1988).

V. A. Howard, *Artistry: The Work of Artists* (Indianapolis: Hackett, 1982).

V. A. Howard and J. H. Barton, *Thinking on Paper* (New York: William Morrow, 1986).

David Hume, *Treatise of Human Nature*, ed. L. A. Selby-Bigge (Oxford: Oxford University Press, 1888).

S. M. Kosslyn, "Imagery and Internal Representation", in E. Rosch and B. B. Lloyds, eds., *Cognition and Categorization* (Hillsdale, N. J.: Lawrence Erlbaum, 1978).

S. M. Kosslyn, T. M. Ball, and B. J. Reiser, "Visual Images Preserve Metric Spatial Information: Evidence from Studies of Image Scanning", *Journal of Experimental Psychology: Human Perception and Performance*, vol. 4 (1978), pp. 47-60.

S. M. Kosslyn, *Ghosts in the Mind's Machine: Creating and Using Images in the Brain* (New York: W. W. Norton, 1983).

W. V. O. Quine, *Word and Object* (Cambridge: MIT Press, 1960).

Gilbert Ryle, *The Concept of Mind* (Chicago: University of Chicago Press, 1984); first published in 1949.

Robert Schwartz, "Imagery—There's More to it than Meets the Eye", *Philosophy of Science Association Proceedings*, vol. 2 (1980), pp. 285-301.

Roger Scruton, *Art and Imagination* (London: Methuen, 1974).

Mary Warnock, *Imagination* (Berkeley: University of California Press, 1978).

PART II
WAYS OF LEARNING

5

Learning by Instruction

On another occasion, in preceptorial, Christian asked me, "Where do you think our ideas come from—justice, righteousness, beauty and so on?" I replied, "Out of the imaginations of men"; and he surprised me by answering, "That is correct".
> —Edmund Wilson on his teacher, Christian Gauss

The Asymmetry of Teaching, Learning, and Instruction

In this chapter I want to survey the landscape of learning by instruction. What is instruction? What are its relations to teaching and learning? Is instruction a rote, authoritative process as contrasted with the more critical kinds of teaching? Is it confined to particular skills? Such titles as drill instructor, driving instructor, swimming instructor would suggest as much. But then, there are religious instructions and packing instructions neither of which have much to do with imparting skills; and packing instructions come without an attached instructor and aim not at learning but at safety. Still, teachers spend a lot of their time instructing, and a lot of instruction does in fact aim at learning. So we are confronted with a range of instructional phenomena that require some sorting out with regard to learning by instruction. Philosophers have mostly ignored the concept of instruction while saying a good deal about the relations of teaching and learning. We may begin with those relations speaking indifferently, for the moment, of instructing or teaching by one person of another.

Clearly, we learn many things without explicit instruction or teaching by another; and while the concept of teaching implies the *intention* that something be learned, nothing guarantees the success of the effort. (Scheffler, 1960, p. 71; Passmore, 1980, p. 20) Nor will it surprise anyone on the teaching end of the learning seesaw that much gets learned that was never intended. That may vary from whatever is communicated "between the lines" by involuntary example or innuendo to plain error and misinterpretation. Even written instructions like recipes for chocolate cake or assembly instructions for a stereo system require to be understood as well as read—which is to say, *interpreted*. And therein recurs a leading theme of the preceding pages; namely, that nothing is given by teaching or instruction that is not also taken, or mistaken.

Accordingly, the domain of learning far exceeds the range of deliberate instruction or of teaching generally to include prejudices, falsehoods, and bad habits; for they also are learned. Consequently, instruction—and more that passes under the label of 'teaching'—concerns as much the unlearning of bad habits, false beliefs, and unsound procedures as the learning of good habits, accurate information, and sound procedures. This fact will surface again when we consider the details of learning by practice. For now, I want to turn to certain asymmetries between teaching and instruction.

Consider that we readily speak of teaching someone to understand physics, to appreciate music, to swim; but there is something awkward about instructing someone to understand physics, to appreciate music, even to swim—almost as if we could order someone to understand or to appreciate. (We can order someone to swim, but that is not the same as instructing him in swimming.) What is missing from the verb phrase 'instruct to' is the adverb 'how'. We normally say that Jones instructs Smith *how* to swim; and it makes equal sense to say that we have been instructed how to understand physics or how to appreciate music—that we have been shown how or that particular procedures have been passed on to us that enable us to understand or to appreciate.

The grammatical difference reflects several conceptual differences. Teaching can be more oblique, inadvertent, or unawares than instruction and includes such indirect modes of influence as involuntary example or suggestion. For instance, it makes sense to say, "His family taught him to be greedy without even trying", where no one deliberately taught him to be greedy or issued specific instructions in the fine art of greediness. And even where teaching is deliberate and involves instruction it remains the broader concept. One can, for instance, alter a person's understanding by instruction, but not necessarily by issuing instructions, and certainly not by the imperative, "Understand!" Instruction, on the other hand, tends to be deliberate, explicit (though not always), and to carry imperative force; which is to say *inter alia* that one can teach something unintentionally but not instruct unintentionally. If it is not a contradiction to say, "Mary's music teacher taught her stage presence quite unawares", it comes close to contradiction to say that her teacher *instructed* her in stage presence quite unawares. The mass noun, 'instruction' is flexible but not so flexible as 'teaching'.

Instruction *versus* Instructions

If there can be teaching without instruction, can there be instruction without instructions? Two things suggest the possibility: first is the fact that so much teaching is *subtle* instruction, a kind of "leading on", as it were; second is the fact that 'instruction' is a mass noun, whereas "instructions" is a so-called count noun, a case of divided reference.[1] That is, you can ask, How many instructions? but not, How many instruction?

Together, these two circumstances indicate that as teaching is more oblique than instruction, so instruction may be more oblique than instructions. In other words, although instruction (the mass noun) is always teaching, instructions (the count noun) are not always teaching. The intermediate case would be one of teaching by instruction without instructions. Israel Scheffler suggests the following anecdote from his own early education. He describes an art instructor with the unnerving habit of wandering about the studio observing his students' work who would suddenly descend upon one of them and wordlessly make a thumb smudge on the student's drawing. He offered no specific advice, no directives, nothing like, "Change this line here, this way". Though unexplicit, the deliberate, imperative force of the thumb smudge is apparent. Other examples of verbally silent or nonlinguistic instruction come to mind as when a dancer, mathematician, or shipwright makes a point to the novice by a simple stroke of the hand, chalk, or adze. In such cases, instruction without denumerable instructions is tantamount to what educators are fond of calling the "discovery method". No specific directive or coded equivalent of a verbal imperative need appear in such situations that could be described as *an* instruction. The learner is expected to find rather than passively to take the point, whatever it happens to be.

Conversely, many examples of instructions without instruction come to mind, some of them mentioned above: recipes, assembly instructions, travel directions, tax forms, safety measures, operating instructions, etc. Though one must learn them to use them, it is not the case that everywhere there are instructions there is a teacher or a concern for teaching.

In sum, while teaching without instruction represents a limiting case at one extreme, most teaching involves instruction and instructions, though teaching by instruction without specific instructions is not uncommon. Finally, at the opposite extreme from teaching without instruction is instructions without instruction or teaching.

If the foregoing analysis fairly represents the ranges and relations among the concepts of teaching, instruction, instructions, and learning, it raises further questions about just how explicit instruction, and instructions, must be and whether all instruction(s) finally reduce to verbal imperatives of the form, "Do this!"

Verbal and Nonverbal Instruction

On the question of how explicit instruction must be, we have already seen that some forms of instruction are not only implicit (unstated) but nonexplicit, which is to say, vague and inviting. The leading question, gesture, or signal may all fall into this category. I recall the seemingly inscrutable gesture-signal of a voice teacher of mine who tapped my chest bone with her fore finger whenever I exhibited strain in the high vocal registers. I eventually figured out that this was intended to draw my attention to the sensation of vibration in the area of the chest bone when the voice is properly placed, supported, and the larynx is anchored downwards. Had she tried to spell all that out in specific directives, not only would the moment be lost (for the music moves on), but I would likely never have gotten the message.

But just how unexplicit was that message? From my point of view at the time it was most vague. But from my teacher's standpoint it was most explicit. What this difference in perspective shows is that instruction that is both deliberate and explicit from the teacher's standpoint does not imply either that it is necessarily verbal or a matter of giving *an* instruction. My teacher's tapping gesture recommended several things to my attention more or less willy-nilly—at least from the standpoint of my asking, "What exactly does she mean by that?" On the other hand, giving *an* instruction, I should maintain, does imply a verbal imperative or its coded equivalent. This requires some explanation.

Giving *an* instruction or instructions amounts to a direct imperative or series of imperatives to the effect, "Do this, and this, and now this!" Instructional imperatives vary in complexity, obviously, and may take the form of simple or elaborate statements written or uttered. On the other hand, we have the examples aforementioned of the choreographer, the mathematician, and the shipwright making a point by a stroke of the hand, chalk, or adze. Previously, I treated such nonverbal signals as broadly suggestive in the manner of the art teacher's smudge gesture or my voice teacher's tapping gesture. But they could well be highly specific in any given instance roughly equivalent to saying, "Make exactly this change here, now."

Note, however, that the symbolisation involved is of two kinds. First, there is the coded equivalent of the verbal imperative, "Do this!" embodied in, say, the shipwright's cut with the adze accompanied perhaps by a significant look in the eyes. Second, there is the cut itself as exemplifying[2] the precise nature of the cut to be made. In other words, this is no ordinary cut; it is simultaneously a coded imperative and a sample of what is to be done. It is a classic instance of "show and tell" complete with bi-directional reference.[3] As the coded equivalent of a verbal imperative, it substitutes for the sentence, "Do this!" denoting the action in question. A less taciturn instructor might even say, "Do this!", but for reasons of efficiency or subtle influence, or simply to avoid distraction, he may prefer the silent version. As a sample action, the cut is self-referential, exhibiting its own properties to the learner who, in the circumstances, is expected to know to which of them to attend.

Other instances of nonverbal instructions function less as samples or demonstrations than as sentence surrogates or coded equivalents of imperatives. Examples would include a conductor's cueing gestures in a musical performance, a sergeant major's frowning at a recruit's unpolished buttons, nodding yes or no, pictorial road signs, highlighted maps showing which route to take, traffic lights, assembly diagrams, and so on. Like the farmer's simply pointing in the direction of the nearest town, the nonverbal directive may be the quickest or easiest or most compelling way to get the point across. And like the conductor's silent gestures, church bells and fog horns have certain dynamic advantages over the spoken word.

To sum up, that part of instruction which consists in the issuing of instructions is in principle verbally expressible so far as its imperative force and some description of what is to be done are concerned, even where the whole is delivered in nonverbal form. That is, *an* instruction is explicit either in words as an imperative or its coded equivalent. This is not true, I have argued, of all instruction, still less of all teaching where the powers of suggestion and of example speak louder than any words.

The Authority of Instruction

One meaning of authority, as any dictionary tells us, is an accepted source of expert information. Relative to that notion, it is one thing to be authoritative, quite another to be authoritarian. Information or instruction that is authoritative arises from a reliable authority or source. To be authoritarian, however, suggests absolute obedience to authority in the sense of established power. Unfortunately, instruction is often portrayed as inherently authoritarian, not merely authoritative—a matter of blindly following orders. Such a view of instruction construes it as an inferior form of teaching leaving little or no room for query, critical response, or reflection.

R. F. Dearden resists this view of instruction as inherently authoritarian as follows.

> On hearing the word 'instruction', we may form a picture of a browbeat-
> ing, hectoring, offensive teacher of a sort admittedly sufficiently
> common in the past to have formed a public stereotype, and in rejecting
> this *picture* we may think that we have validly rejected all instruction. But
> that would be so only if it could first be shown that all instruction must
> necessarily be of this bullying and insensitive kind. A further feature of
> this picture which is no necessary accompaniment of instruction is that
> of baldly telling someone something . . . so that things are learned by
> rote. Instruction *need* not be confined to such bald exposition of various
> items of information, but may include a reasoned explanation of some-
> thing or an experimental demonstration of it . . . Again, instruction *need*
> not be given by word of mouth, but may be given by referring the
> learner to a lesson in a textbook . . . Far from being tied to some particu-
> lar form which the accident of tradition has given to it, instruction may
> take many forms and be given in more than one manner. (Dearden,
> 1967, pp. 137-138)

That about says it on the topic of authoritarian instruction
except to note that one sense of the verb 'to instruct' is 'to
order' as in "The magistrate instructed me to come to his
office". The senses of 'instruction' and 'instructions' that I have
been considering here also carry imperative force but not in the
form of blind or punishable orders (on pain of . . .). The
authority of instructional orders ideally rests in sources of
expertise and reliable information rather than threats of
punishment. As well, instructions may also take the form of
recipes, directions, or suggestions entirely without the implica-
tion of sanctions of the kind attached, say, to military
commands.

Far from being categorical morally or coercively, instructional
commands are conditional and prudential in the sense of, "If
you want to learn how to do this well, then you must undertake
the following." That places primary responsibility on the adult
learner (and on whomever has responsibility for the child
learner) to find and to follow authoritative sources of expertise.
By the same token, the primary responsibility of the instructor
or author of instructions is to *be* an authoritative source of
expertise.

Dearden on Instruction

While I agree with Dearden on the question of authoritarian
instruction, I disagree with his account of the cognitive and sym-

bolic aspects of instruction. His views deserve careful consideration and help to clarify my own.

Dearden writes, "If we ask what is distinctive of instruction as a way of passing on knowledge, the answer would seem to be that in instruction this knowledge is directly imparted." (Dearden, 1978, p. 138) Even were we to ignore those intermediate cases of indirect instruction cited above (e.g., the thumb smudging and chest tapping cases), that is already ignoring too much of what goes under the label of instruction. I presume that Dearden is referring to denumerable instructions here, overlooking the flexibility of the mass noun, 'instruction'. This assumption is borne out by what he goes on to say: "Instruction does not hint at, or seek to elicit, or guide one in finding out for oneself, but directly imparts, and hence in this respect stands in sharp contrast as a way of teaching to contriving that children learn by discovery." (p. 138)

I disagree both that instruction does not hint and that it excludes discovery. In the first place, instruction can be highly suggestive and "leading" as we have seen. Secondly, even explicit instructions, particularly those of the "show and tell" variety discussed above require an interpretive effort on the part of the learner. However minimal, the interpretive activity of the learner *is* discovery; and inasmuch as instructional samples and demonstrations do not "speak" for themselves except as they are selectively construed within a context, innumerable small acts of discovery are ingredient to learning from instruction.

Dearden appears to fall prey here to the myth of the given, the idea that certain things are passively impressed upon the mind or body. That may be so *relatively* speaking, that is, compared to higher levels of thought, imagination, or action. But the fact remains that learning begins in and never leaves the realms of discovery and imagination insofar one must grasp the meaning of the hints, cues, examples, or explicit directions proffered. Otherwise, nothing *new* should ever be found out by instruction, and that is contrary to fact.

Dearden goes on to examine a famous case of what he considers to be teaching without instruction.

In Plato's dialogue the *Meno*, Socrates teaches a slave that a square double the area of a given square is to be constructed on the diagonal of the given square, and not by doubling the length of its sides, but he does not actually impart this information: he elicits it. At one point he comments to Meno as follows:

'Now notice what, starting from this state of perplexity, he will discover by seeking the truth in company with me . . . Be ready to catch me if I give him any instruction or explanation instead of simply interrogating him on his own opinions'.

Though all instruction may require the use of language, then, not all teaching by the use of language is instruction, and though this may seem obvious enough once it has been pointed out, it has nevertheless escaped the notice of the more extreme reactionaries against the teacher as instructor . . . (pp. 138-139)

First off, note that the phrase "any instruction" is ambiguous between instruction (the mass noun) and instructions (the count noun). The disjunctive phrase, "or explanation" shifts the emphasis to the count noun, instructions. Socrates could fairly be said not to have given any instructions (explanations, directives) to the slave. But has he not given instruction in the form of leading questions? Of course he has, and with precisely the objective of showing how the slave can discover for himself the solution of the problem. Socrates did what Scheffler's art instructor and my voice teacher did, namely, put the learner in the way of knowledge and a better understanding of what is required to solve the problem at hand. Such guidance is the quintessence of instruction at its most flexible and insightful. Hence, I cannot agree that Socrates' encounter with the slave is an instance of teaching without instruction, or that instruction *reduces* to "teaching by telling". (p. 139)

On the point that "all instruction may require the use of language [but] not all teaching by the use of language is instruction", (p. 139) I agree with the latter clause (and with Dearden's observation about "reactionaries") but not with the antecedent clause. Though most instruction involves the use of language, and in the case of denumerable instructions the coded equivalents of language, nonverbal forms of instruction are commonplace as we have seen. I prefer to say that all instruction(s) involves symbolisation, some form of reference, in a wide variety of symbolic systems: gestural, graphic, pictorial, notational, linguistic, including exemplificational reference as in samples, demonstrations, and illustrations. Broadening the domains of meaning and of interpretation beyond language has the twin advantages, first, of providing for the interaction of language with other symbolic systems and illustrative actions in instruction and, second, of avoiding the reduction of instruction to "telling".

On the topic of skills, Dearden remarks that "where *skill* is concerned . . . intelligent instruction . . . together with practice, would seem to be quite the best way of teaching, and we may notice that wherever a teaching job is specifically that of passing on such a skill we do talk of 'instructors', such as driving, gunnery and flying instructors, or instructors in the various crafts." (p. 139) He further notes the role of instruction in the acquisition and mastery of "concepts, principles and criteria of critical appraisal" in subjects not normally regarded as "skills" such as mathematics and history. Far from treating them as "collections of information", he argues, "there is no reason at all why proofs, evidences and arguments could not be made the content of instruction quite as much as what they are the reasons for." To which he adds the coda, "So long as there is something definite to be imparted, then it can be made the content of instruction." (pp. 139-140)

It is difficult to see how "proofs, evidences, and arguments" as ingredient to instruction in the academic disciplines (and possibly in skill instruction?) can be made consistent with his claim one page earlier that instruction comes down to "teaching by telling". Logically, Dearden appears to shift his ground here from talking about "instructions" to the broader conception of "instruction" in order to accommodate the role of instruction in the disciplines, limiting it, quite rightly I think, to "something definite to be imparted".

In the very next paragraph, however, Dearden shifts back to the narrower conception of instruction where he says, "If not just memorization of the content of instruction is desirable, but an intelligent mastery of it, involving judgement in its application, then instruction cannot be wholly adequate." (p. 140) Rather, instruction at a skill or an academic discipline needs to be "supplemented by practice" to allow for the growth of judgement in applying either the skill or the concepts, principles, and criteria of the discipline "in a suitable variety of cases". This, he concludes, is instruction "at its most intelligent . . . from the point of view of knowledge and passing on that knowledge." (p. 140)

Here again Dearden shifts from the narrower to the broader conception of instruction within a few sentences, from a view that places practice outside the scope of instruction to one that includes it. No doubt practice plays an important role not only as a supplement to instruction but as a part of it. That is, practice itself requires close scrutiny and supervision. (See Chapter 6 below.) And no doubt practice "in a suitable variety of cases" contributes substantially to the growth of judgement in applying what one learns by instruction, including self-instruction. But it is difficult to see how "just memorization of the content of instruction" could be any more than the barest starting point of that development, nor yet how that development could be sustained except by the more generous view of instruction as involving reasons, explanations, and evidences.

In sum, Dearden appears to confound the count noun 'instructions' and the mass noun 'instruction' throughout his discussion shifting back and forth from one to the other: from the notion of instruction as "teaching by telling" *simpliciter* to instruction as involving reasons, explanations, and even practice. The effect is to obscure the more oblique forms of instruction, on the one hand, and the role of discovery in instruction generally, on the other. Instruction as essentially "telling" further obscures the nonlinguistic symbolic systems involved at all levels of instruction. On the positive side of the ledger, Dearden rightly criticizes the notion of instruction as inherently authoritarian. As well, he clarifies the role of instruction in teaching the academic disciplines and draws attention to the link with practice as furthering the growth of judgement.

Following Instructions: the Beginning

In the second half of this survey of learning by instruction, I want to examine the humble beginnings of all instruction by asking, What is it to *follow* instructions? How do we get from halting adherence to precept and rule to fluid performance? What changes occur in that passage, and how might we describe them?

A first preliminary point to be made is that following instructions is not the same as following orders blindly or passively like obeying military commands or "going through the motions". Obeisance of either of those kinds depends upon extrinsic motives: the avoidance of sanctions, or the fear of giving offense, or to save appearances. Following instructions, on the other hand, is predicated on *justifiable trust* that the proffered rules and directions will achieve some desired result. (Black, 1968, p. 95) Such confidence is an intrinsic motive tied directly to the presumed efficacy of the instructions themselves. Who would follow untrustworthy instructions except, perhaps, to save face or to demonstrate their failure? In other words, instructions are, as noted above, (p. 67) conditional and prudential, justified by their actual or presumed success in getting certain results.

A second preliminary point is that following instructions is an *intentional* effort, an action consciously undertaken, not mere "behaviour" or something that happens to us—however much of what we actually do turns out to be accidental or unintended. The measure of acceptance of an instructional imperative is that one actually obeys it, tries to follow it. It is not enough merely to say, "I accept these instructions" and then do nothing or act contrary to them. Following instructions, therefore, enlists both the confidence and the *active* consent of the learner.

As we have seen, instructions may take the form of an explicit series of steps to be executed that virtually anybody could follow, or they may come as elusive, often implicit, "tips and cues" that only highly trained individuals could follow. Eric Satie, for instance, somewhere in one of his chamber pieces left instructions that it be played "like a nightingale with a toothache". Be it doing things by rote, by cue, or by subtle suggestion, such behaviour is a compound of precept and action that philosophers since Wittgenstein call "rule governed" or "rule following" action. (Wittgenstein, 1953, pp. 80-81) My concern is with the nature of the "following"—how the learner absorbs and applies rules—which varies with the types of rules, the perspectives from which they are articulated, and the levels of their mastery.

The notion of rule itself is notoriously vague and a matter of continuing philosophical debate. I shall use the term in its broadest sense as an authoritative direction for conduct or procedure inclusive of recipes, standard routines, "tips and cues", directions, and other so-called practical principles. Space permits only passing attention to the subtle differences among the latter while focussing on the question of what it is to follow and to be guided by rules of these kinds. To my knowledge, over the past twenty years only two philosophers, Max Black and Andrew Harrison, have addressed the *pedagogical* issue of following instructions directly and in detail, the former in a well known article, "Rules and Routines" (1968) and the latter in Chapter 5 of his *Making and Thinking* (1978) entitled, "Recipes and Practical Pedantry".[4] Though separated by ten years, the two pieces are quite complementary, so I will consider them together in this and the concluding section.

Black is concerned with the basic types of rule-governed action, while Harrison focuses mainly upon the cognitive, interpretive demands of following and applying rules and recipes. Let us start with Black.

An action is *rule-invoking*, in Black's terminology, if it follows a set of explicit, fully articulated procedures or steps, as in a drill manual, any one of which steps could be invoked by the agent to justify or explain what he or she is doing at a given moment. (Black, 1968, p. 97) In heeding them, one is fully aware of the rules exactly as stated or written out; that is, one could recite or read them off at the appropriate times: "Now I am doing this, and now that," etc. Familiar examples would include traffic regulations, exercise regimes, cookbooks, military commands, medical prescriptions, tax forms, legal restrictions, and the like. Ignoring other factors, all that is required is a set of directions and the will to follow them.

Such appeal to a precept to explain one's action differs from mere routine or regular behaviour in having a reason, in the ability to say what one is doing and why. (p. 97) It is the difference, say, between putting on one's trousers right leg first (for which there may be no "reason" that one would care to cite as a precept other than sheer habit) and citing a rule that explains, justifies, or states the motive of one's action. As Black says, "Reasons for actions are typically offered to defend or to justify the actions; to render them intelligible; or to amplify their descriptions by reference to intention, motive, or purpose". (p. 97)

Looking in the other direction, however, not so much towards justifying or explaining one's actions (important as these are) but towards *applying* a precept or rule, the question arises as to the difference between slavish adherence to precept and the interpretation of precept according to conditions. In other words, what differences are worth noting between a rule-focussed and a world-focussed approach to following instructions?

As Harrison observes, even where one knows what one wants and has before him instructions for reaching that goal, "there may still be a question, which is very like a question of rationality, about his practical good sense in how he follows the recipe. For it is possible to follow a recipe well or badly, with block-headed pedantry or with ease and grace. Just as there is more to playing music than playing the notes, so there is more to following any instruction for achieving a repeatable effect than reading it, marking it, even learning it and putting it into practice." (Harrison, 1978, p. 70)

The analogy of a musical score is apt, for it too is a "recipe" for "the repetition of a certain result" (p. 71) notwithstanding the latitude it allows for interpretive imagination and performance artistry. Though such latitude may be ever so much greater for a musical score than for the average cookbook recipe, it would be "wrong to conclude from this that to a similar, if a more humble, extent very much the same does not apply to what it is to follow any recipe. No recipe can itself contain instructions for how it should be followed. Some element of invention[5] must be involved in following any recipe." (p. 71)

If in justifying or explaining our actions we are more rule-focussed, then in applying instructions we are more world-focussed. An important aspect of that world focus is having, or developing, a "feel" for the materials to which the rules apply. Such "feeling" is, in Scheffler's phraseology, a "cognitive emotion". (Scheffler, 1981) That is, the feeling that a singer has for the voice, a sculptor for certain stones or metals, a carpenter for woods, is very much an emotional-physical affection. Beyond that, however, such feelings are cognitive, engaging the understanding in many ways. "A 'feeling for materials'", says Harrison, "is a feeling right enough, but is a feeling that directs *attention* and concentrates choice and judgement in a particular and often highly specific manner, and these are intellectual matters." (p. 74)

As with drill and other humble routines, a primary goal of instructions is to acquaint the learner with the "materials" (one might broadly say the domain) of application of the rules invoked. (Recall once again Mme. Nilsson's salient instructions to Mr. Barth in Chapters 2 and 3.) To that extent, the more "practical" the rule, the more world-focussed it is, the greater the demands upon our rational, interpretive capacities, and, as Harrison rightly observes, "the greater the danger, and absurdity of, pedantry in its use." (p. 76)

To return to Black's taxonomy: an action is *rule-accepting* if a rule could be formulated that precisely describes what one is dong even if one is not consciously aware of it. It is matter of what a person can accept as an accurate account of what he is doing. It is essential, Black says, that the rule "seem obvious" and its acceptance by the agent be unhesitating. "The harder it is to formulate the rule, and the more reluctant the agent is to accept it, the less inclined we ought to be to treat the episode as a clear case of rule-acceptance." (p. 98) For example, if I am observed to be tapping my foot in time with the *Skater's Waltz*, someone might say, "Ah, I see that you are counting the meter in 3/4 time." "Yes", I might reply, if indeed I were. Or, "No, I'm not *counting* at all; it's just reflex—I don't even know what 3/4 time means".

Though Black does not say so, implicit in this situation is the condition of rule rejection: of being able to say what one is *not* doing. Similarly, one must be prepared to reject the action too once the "rule" is presented negatively in such a statement as, "You took your eye off the ball again". "Ah, yes, I'll try to do better next time". The rejection of either rule or action here depends upon one's ability to assess the action in question as an instance or not of the description proffered.

One other caveat. The requirements that the rule seem obvious to the agent and be unhesitatingly accepted could be misleading on two counts. First, it may take some time for the "diagnosis" to sink in as in many cases of therapy and coaching. A considerable amount of trial and error practice and self-monitoring (under supervision) may be required even to *see* that a particular rule applies or is being broken. Second, the diagnosis could be wrong and yet be accepted by the agent, as in all too common cases of authoritarian instruction. Allowance needs be made for intimidating circumstances where the learner is predisposed to accept uncritically anything the instructor says.

Having noted these provisos, rule-accepting action represents a major port of entry for diagnostic and critical judgement from without—in effect, an opportunity to discover from those with expertise what in fact we are doing, what is right or wrong about it, and how to improve. To the degree that this is so, rule-accepting action is the place where the instructional languages of craft and of lore[6]—the trade jargons of various kinds of know-how—enter into dialogue with actual practice.

I say "dialogue" because in the act of absorbing the commentary the learner is thrust into an attitude of self-scrutiny and assessment within a means-ends nexus that is anything but fixed. Rather, as described in Chapter 3, the learner is immersed in a Deweyean *continuum* of means and ends that are mutually revisible with increasing comprehension and competence. More specifically, one's understanding of the prescribed or diagnostic rules changes with practice at applying some (invoked rules) and discovering how others (accepted rules) apply to one's actions.

Following Instructions: The Middle and the End

Obviously, not all explanations and rules of action are of a sort that could be "followed". Physical, psychological, or economic explanations, for instance, are typically cast in language that is nondirective and far too complicated for the agent enmeshed in activity to grasp let alone follow. Yet much of our behaviour and deliberate actions "obey", in the sense of are covered by, such rules as, for example, the gambler's variable-ratio schedule of reinforcement. According to Black, an action is *rule-covered* wherever "an outside analyst can give a certain kind of description of it—can view it *sub specie regulae*, as it were." (p. 99)

The notion of a rule that "covers" in the sense of explaining or describing an action without necessarily directing it marks the difference between theoretical understanding (or "propositional" knowledge) and knowing-how (or "procedural" knowledge). (See Ryle, 1949, Ch. 2; Scheffler, 1965, Ch. 5; Howard, 1982, p. 49)

Though contingently related in innumerable ways, their logical independence is shown by the fact that neither one implies the other. Polanyi's famous example is that knowing how to ride a bicycle may be explained as a constant adjustment of the curvature of the bicycle's path in proportion to the ratio of the unbalance over the square of the speed. (Polanyi, 1958, p. 50) Clearly, knowing that bit of physics is neither necessary nor sufficient to learning how to ride—and conversely. Again, such an explanation cites a rule that covers (by explaining) without directing action. A covering rule's influence is therefore indirect, resulting, perhaps, in revisions of practical directives or confirming others in that relation we call "theory to practice".

Before such rules can become pedagogically useful, they require "translation" into the language of instruction, usually in terms of their effects. "Turn the wheel in the direction of the unbalance! Why? Because, that will prevent you from falling over." The logical relations between theoretical explanations and practical directives are complicated, particularly where the latter derive from or are "corrected" by the former as in the bearing of studies of child development on teaching or sport physiology on coaching techniques. I have dealt with some of those relations elsewhere.[7] It suffices here only to say that practical directives of either the invoking or accepting kind often encapsulate the hybrid fruits of covering (theoretical) explanations and sometimes centuries of practical lore.

Regarding the bearing of covering rules on action, Black says, "This kind of verbal articulation is of no value by way of 'self-criticism', to the agent himself, though it may have considerable importance elsewhere", e.g., in computer or robot simulations of human activity. (p. 99) As a blanket claim, "no value" is tantamount to denying that theory of any kind could have any bearing on practice. In fairness, Black probably means no *immediate* value by way of self-criticism to the agent. The point is worth picking up, however, because covering rules can have great self critical value to the agent *retrospectively* in seeking a deeper understanding of the success or failure of his own actions.

Covering rules have an even greater value to those who instruct. Were I to direct someone trying to learn to ride a bicycle to turn the wheel away from the direction of the unbalance, Polanyi's little bit of physics would prove me wrong. And as much in its way as the inevitable fall, it would show *why* the advice is wrong. Similarly, much recent work in voice physiology, for instance, has rejuvenated and confirmed the healthy practices of the older *bel canto* techniques of voice training. (Cf. Husler and Rodd-Marling, 1976) Even wider ranging examples are readily come by. Advances in sport physiology and kinesiology, in learning theory, in symbol theory and language development all have had profound influence upon training and educational practice. The facts that such influence is indirect (covering), piecemeal and complex, and usually delayed hardly amounts to "no value" to the struggling learner. Quite the contrary, the diagnostic uses of such knowledge to teachers, coaches, and therapists are incalculable.

A minor puzzle is that rule-accepting and rule-covering actions are not necessarily distinct on Black's formulation, i.e., a rule-covering explanation also exactly describes what one is doing and therefore *could* be rule-accepting. For example, "Increase the angular velocity!" just might make sense as a directive to a baseball pitcher who knows something about the physics of levers. However, talk of a rule that *could* be followed is ambiguous between one that *is* followed, descriptively, and one that can be *appealed to*, acceptingly, in the first person, as effective to direct or to improve performance. For any rule, covering or not, its acceptance, solely for reasons of comprehension, will vary from one person to another and from time to time. And some rules will forever remain much too complicated for citation *in medias res*. That is perhaps a contingent matter, but the "appeal" proviso for rule-accepting actions is sufficient to keep them at least psychologically distinct from rule-covered actions.

The last category in Black's taxonomy is *rule-guided* action, where, in lieu of explicit, stated directives, we find only "tips and cues", including imagery and other nonverbal versions amounting to a "phenomenological compression" of vast amounts of detail in a "reduction to essentials". (p. 100) By this stage of following instructions, attempts at "'verbal articulation' may be disconcertingly difficult . . . arising out of the agent's "use of a private symbolism of visual [or other nonverbal] cues, that has ousted the public and official terminology of the original instructions." (p. 100)

A distinguishing feature of this "assimilated" level of action is an ease and fluency of execution conspicuously absent from the jerky spectacle of consulting rules one by one. What synoptic shorthand as one devises or is given for rendering things down to their essentials is "appropriately articulated by non-verbal symbolism" in a kind of "intuitive transformation or 'condensation'". In the interest of fluency, this is a "necessary effort to impose a memorable order upon what looks initially like a chaos of unrelated items." (p. 101)

Though intuitively transformed and idiosyncratic, such "condensations", Black urges, are "not 'private' in the philosopher's technical sense of unintelligibility in principle to another". (p. 100) Indeed they are not; nor are they always personally private either. For it is just such mnemonic, controlling devices as constitute the "tips" and "cues" that one may offer another to guide the exercise of high skill. This raises the orthogonal question whether such nonverbal "condensations" are always reducible in principle to statable versions.

Wittgenstein, for one, places such subtle hints beyond the realm of rules and formulae altogether (Wittgenstein, 1953, p. 60), whereas Black views them as simplified, though amazingly versatile *summaries* of rules, the means whereby "*the* rule" becomes "*my* rule" in a fluid performance. (p. 101) Both acknowledge, while I have stressed, their role in directing, thinking and communicating about the subtleties of skill. It is just here, at the rule-guided level, that following instructions becomes an increasingly autonomous activity mediated by "heuristic imagery" of the sort described in Chapter 4. It would appear, therefore, that a complete account of the "phenomenological compression" characteristic of rule-guided action would acknowledge all these permutations of the imagination at work: within and beyond specified rules and routines and in a variety of symbolic systems.

Between the extremes of blind effort, rule-covered action, and slavish adherence to precept, rule-invoking action, Black locates the relative ease of implicit conformity to rule (rule-accepting action) and the free flowing action without apparent calculation of trained mastery (rule-guided action). On Black's view, the foregoing sequence represents an "ideal cycle, indefinitely repeated". (p. 102) As we have already seen, not all instructions aim at learning let alone independent judgement; so we may safely presume that Black's "ideal cycle" applies to those world-focussed instructions that aim not merely to explain, justify, or direct, but at autonomous, skillful performance guided by judgement and choice.

The point I should like to emphasize in this connection is that however one describes the phases of learning by instruction, the full cycle of development from novice to expert, from dependency to autonomy, takes the form of training that is symbolically mediated even if, as must happen, there comes a time for casting rules aside.

This in turn suggests that there are limitations on the articulation of rules beyond those arising either from an inability to put things into words (or other symbols) or from the initial obscurity to the agent of such formulations.

Consider the following situation. A standard tax form instructs us to "enter all taxable income". The form then supplies rules for determining what is taxable income. We can imagine further rules for interpreting the rules for determining taxable income, and so on indefinitely. What stops the regress of rules? In a word, unintelligibility. "The chain of rules", says Black, "will quickly terminate, for want of an adequate vocabulary. The nearer we come to what is readily *seen* by an apt learner, the harder it becomes to articulate the governing rule and a point is soon reached at which the effort of attending to the verbal formula positively interferes with the primary performance." (p. 101)

Now this interference is not the unintelligibility of misuse, mistiming, or first encounter with a new terminology, but of distraction. It is a case of excessively rule-focussed instruction wherein language outstrips its directive usefulness almost to the point of trying to *reproduce* the prescribed behaviour. Harrison makes a similar point where he speaks of "how 'rough' or otherwise the descriptions in the principle should be taken to be. But it is misleading to see this as if it were a matter of paying attention to the *principle*. It is a matter of paying attention to the world it must be applied in." (Harrison, 1978, p. 75) "Of course," Black remarks, "sensible men soon abandon *saying* in favour of *showing*." (p. 102)

And so they do; not only, however, to avoid the distraction of verbal overload, but also because one quickly reaches the point where a single example, demonstration, or image may be far more *symbolically* instructive of "how to" than any description. The notion of "what is readily *seen* by an apt learner" is still a matter of interpretive guidance.

Learning by example is the subject of a later chapter. For now, it suffices to say that the two parts of "show and tell" pedagogy are bound together not merely by the limitations of linguistic description but by a common instructional purpose within a symbolic nexus—a bit like looking at maps of a given terrain, reading descriptions of it, and visiting the area in order to form an opinion of what it is "really" like. Briefly put, abandoning descriptions and rules for demonstrations and samples is less a jettisoning of symbols than a shift in their emphasis or "direction". And that observation leads naturally on to the topic of the next chapter, namely, how we learn by practice.

The message of this chapter has been that learning by instruction generally or by specific instructions is anything but a passive affair; that the various functions of symbols and the necessity of interpretation stalk the effort every step of the way. Beginning with the learner's confidence in particular instructions and consent to be guided by them, critical intelligence is required both to understand and to apply them. From written recipes and directions to the subtle interventions of an imaginative teacher, the learner is plunged by instruction into a symbolic welter of means-ends thinking that alerts mind and body to possible options even as it trains them to "follow the rules".

Notes

1 W. V. O. Quine, *Word and Object* (Cambridge: MIT Press, 1960), pp. 90-95.

2 Exemplification is a technical term in symbol theory. It is defined as a subset of the converse of denotation. A paint sample of Mink White, for instance, exemplifies the label, 'Mink White' which denotes the sample. See Goodman, *Languages of Art*, pp. 52-57.

3 For an extensive discussion of the varieties of "show and tell", see *Artistry*, pp. 99-109.

4 Philosophical studies of rules and rule-governed behaviour in language, morals, and action theory are legion but of peripheral relevance to the present discussion. Michael Polanyi's examination of skills in Chapter 4 of his *Personal Knowledge* (1958) is tangential and will be considered in following chapters. Also relevant is Thomas F. Green's acute analysis of "Teaching, Acting, and Behaving" (1964) along with the commentaries of Jonas R. Soltis, R. S. Peters, James E. McClellan, and a reply by Green (1965).

5 Harrison suggests a rough distinction between 'invention' and 'creativity' (or two kinds of 'inventiveness'): 'invention', he says, "has to do with those cases where the agent 'knows' his goal but not his means", whereas 'creativity' has to do "with the fact that in some central sense the agent is not fully aware of his own goal." (p. 70) I doubt that this characterization of creativity would stand up to scrutiny, but the distinction is nonetheless useful as drawing attention to the mutual indeterminacy of ends and their means.

6 As described in *Artistry*, Chs. 3 & 4.

7 In *Artistry*, Chs. 2, 3, & 4.

References

Max Black, "Rules and Routines" in *The Concept of Education*, ed. R. S. Peters (London: Routledge & Kegan Paul, 1968).

R. F. Dearden, "Instruction and Learning by Discovery", in *The Concept of Education* (London: Routledge & Kegan Paul, 1968).

Nelson Goodman, *Languages of Art, An Approach to a Theory of Symbols* (Indianapolis: Hackett, 1972).

Thomas F. Green, "Teaching, Acting, and Behaving", *Harvard Educational Review*, vol. 34, no. 4 (Fall 1964), pp. 507-524; plus "Discussion" with Jonas R. Soltis, R. S. Peters, James E. McClellan, and Thomas F. Green, *Harvard Educational Review*, vol. 35, no. 2 (Spring 1965), pp. 191-209.

Andrew Harrison, *Making and Thinking* (Indianapolis: Hackett, 1978).

V. A. Howard, *Artistry, The Work of Artists* (Indianapolis: Hackett, 1982).

Frederick Husler and Yvonne Rodd-Marling, *Singing, the Physical Nature of the Vocal Organ* (London: Hutchinson, 1976).

John Passmore, *The Philosophy of Teaching* (Cambridge: Harvard University Press, 1980).

Michael Polanyi, *Personal Knowledge* (London: Routledge & Kegan Paul, 1958).

W. V. O. Quine, *Word and Object* (Cambridge: MIT Press, 1960).

Gilbert Ryle, *The Concept of Mind* (Chicago: University of Chicago Press, 1984); first published in 1949.

Israel Scheffler, *The Language of Education* (Springfield: Charles C. Thomas, 1960).

Israel Scheffler, *The Conditions of Knowledge* (Glenview: Scott, Foresman, 1965; reprinted by the University of Chicago Press, 1986).

Israel Scheffler, "In Praise of the Cognitive Emotions", *Teachers College Record*, vol. 79, no. 2, 1977; reprinted in *Inquiries, Philosophical Studies of Language, Science, and Learning* (Indianapolis: Hackett, 1986).

Ludwig Wittgenstein, *Philosophical Investigations*, tr. G. E. M. Anscombe (Oxford: Blackwell, 1953).

6

Learning by Practice

If a man that is not perfect be ever in practice, he shall as well practice his errors as his abilities and induce one habit of both; and there is no means to help this but by seasonable intermissions.

—Francis Bacon, *Of Nature in Men.*

TIPS for Success

When it comes to the honing of skills and the stamping in of various habits and procedures, nothing beats sound instruction combined with assiduous drill. Practice makes perfect, the saying goes, especially for the highly gifted. Enshrined therein are two of the most commonplace clichés about learning in the English language: that of native talent and its shaping by persistent repetition. Add to talent and practice the watchful direction of an instructor and the formula is complete for success in the classroom, in the artist's studio, or on the playing field. Talent + Instruction + Practice = Success.

Like most common sense generalisations about learning, the TIPS formula is expressed in terms invitingly vague and ambiguous. Variations on TIPS are ubiquitous in educational thought allotting different meanings and weights to each of the three causal terms, 'talent', 'instruction' and 'practice'. For example, some proponents of early aptitude (Seashore, 1947), of IQ or genetically based intelligence (Jensen, 1972, 1981) and personality factors (Kagen and Brim, 1980) tend to stress the "givens" of human nature in learning. On the other hand, while disagreeing on most other matters, behavioural and cognitive psychologists agree in stressing the "environmental" factors of instruction and practice. (Cf. Skinner, 1965; Bruner, 1986) Interestingly, many art teachers and athletics coaches take the rather self-effacing view that talent (including personality factors like "ambition" and "toughness") plus practice helped along by instructional nudges mostly determine who will or will not succeed.

More puzzling than any of the quarrels among psychologists or practitioners over teaching and learning advanced skills is the reductive approach of so much curriculum research. Aiming at quick results on the basis of an "empirical" interpretation of the TIPS formula, curriculum developers often view their task as three-fold: first, using one set of criteria reduce all questions of gifts or talents to ones of measurable, fixed aptitudes or potentials; second, by another set of criteria reduce all questions of instruction and training to technological ones of sufficient means to specifiable ends; and third, read off the formulae for success from the behaviour of those who have succeeded thereby converting *established* practice into *recommended* practice.[1]

While seeming to temper the wind to the shorn lamb, such tactics end by slaughtering the lamb. Issues of value and choice, of symbolism and interpretation, of judgement and understanding, of inquiry and discovery cannot easily be rendered down. Aside from the obvious confusion of the "is" with the "ought" of prevailing practice, such an approach to learning skills (or anything else for that matter) assumes, first, that potentials and aptitudes are more given than made; second, that they are changeless and nonconflicting in their development; and third, that they are value-free in their higher cultivation and uses. Such an approach to learning is less scientific than scientistic. [2]

That this kind of social science fiction engenders mere "bags of tricks" is hardly noteworthy. What is noteworthy about all the aforementioned variations on the TIPS formula is their inattention to the several roles of imagination in learning; to the conceptual landscape of instruction; to the personal growth of performance standards; to the interpretive effort required to learn from one's mistakes; and most conspicuously, to the nature of practice itself: learning to practice and practising to learn.

The humblest term in the TIPS formula, practice is in fact a complex concept encompassing a range of sophisticated activities from finger drills to dress rehearsal, from rote memorisation to critical strategy. Failure to grasp the subtleties of practice leads to oversimplification as exemplified by the phrase "mere drill", on the one hand, and, on the other, to overreliance on vague notions like gift, talent, knack, or inspiration to explain how advanced skills are mastered. I turn now to some enlightening ambiguities in the notion of practice.

Practice *versus* Practising

Hereinafter, for clarity's sake, I shall modify the spelling convention that distinguishes the noun, as in *a* or *the* practice, from the verb, as in *to* practise or practising. The latter spelling will be artificially restricted to the kinds of repetitive practise involved in training and drill; whereas, the former spelling will be allowed to range over the intermediate cases of exercising an occupation or profession as when we speak of practicing law or medicine. On the proposed usage, doctors practice medicine while medical students practise medicine.

A (the) practice refers to an established or customary way of doing things. That may be a matter of accumulated knowledge and rational precedent as in medicine or law; a matter of arbitrary convention as with left or right drive traffic; a matter of ritual and doctrine as in religious practices; a matter of principle as in moral practices; or a matter of culture as with certain social practices such as bowing or shaking hands. In these and similar instances, *the* practice represents the "done thing", what tradition, ritual, past experience, precedent, or lore bequeaths to us.

We should indeed be deprived without the established practices of the professions, disciplines, arts, and occupations. Such practices take the form of vast natural experiments and comprise the accumulated wisdom of a given field that gets passed on to succeeding generations of practitioners. In other forms, as conventions of etiquette, rules of parliamentary debate, or traffic regulations, established practices make up the "social grease" that facilitates the conduct of everyday life.

Little wonder, then, that practising is often construed as a way of handing on the establishment—of internalising the done thing by drill, itself construed as a kind of obedient, mindless repetition. Examples from reciting multiplication tables to early moral and social conduct to military training readily come to mind as reflexive "second nature" stamped in by drill. Such acquired, automatic behaviour of second nature is seen in turn to capitalise on the innate reactions of "first nature". Embedded in the TIPS formula aforementioned, such a view of practices and practising reinforces the notion of instruction and training as rote processes demanding compliance over critical interpretation. By this route, professional training in virtually any field comes to be seen as an inflexible, blinkered way of passing on established knowledge and procedures. Against this view I shall argue that practise is not limited to passing on *the* practice by drill, and, that even where that is the emphasis, drill is anything but mindless repetition.

I once visited a dental laboratory where student dentists were practising bridge making techniques: bending the tiny wires just so, molding the prosthetic materials, and, incidentally, strengthening their fingers. They did this under the watchful eye of a senior technician himself under the supervision of a dental surgeon. "You cannot afford to make a mistake like this once you are in practice", the technician crooned quietly as he examined a piece of student work. Again and again he gently admonished his students for this or that technical flaw, making corrections as he passed along the bench, so that the flaws and their corrections were instantly clear. Every now and then, he would hold up a piece and exclaim, "Ah, perfect! Exactly right." Only once, three quarters of the way down the bench, did he pick up a piece, shake his head admiringly and say, "I couldn't match this work myself".

A learning situation in which practise converges more on *the* practice could hardly be imagined. Yet even here, the technician acknowledged one student's work as surpassing "the done thing", as exceeding the standards of established practice. Beyond that, the levels of concentration and attention to detail exhibited by the students as they bent over their work could hardly be described as "mindless repetition" however many times they repeated a particular task. The fact that the procedures being practised will eventually become routinised is beside the point. Even military recruits learning to slope arms must initially attend to the task as a precondition of its becoming automatic on command. At the opposite extreme, musical virtuosi continue to practise, often under supervision, long after they have mastered "the done thing", partly to reinforce certain "fundamentals" but mostly to extend established standards of performance. Paradoxically, it takes a lot of thoughtful effort to learn to do something "without thinking".

If then, practise can exceed the limits of *the* practice and drill is more often mindful than mindless, practise also may fail to make perfect in at least two ways: first, the practise may be faulty; second, *the* practice may be faulty. As Francis Bacon reminds us in the epigraph to this chapter, errors and bad habits get stamped in by practise quite as readily as proficiencies unless the former are recognised as such and corrected by "seasonable intermissions". Both Mme. Nilsson from an earlier example and the dental technician above are expert in ferreting out and diagnosing mistakes in ways that make them *evident* to the learner. In short, vigilance and not only repetition is the price of improvement through practise.

Still, vigilance and care may not be enough where *the* practice itself is faulty. Once errors are stamped into the tradition, of established practice, they often are perpetuated with great momentum. Which is to say, that faulty schemas can get built in and made second nature along with, or thwarting, improvements. A generation of singers in the 1930s and 1940s, enthralled by Caruso recordings, mistakenly supposed that his vocal prowess was due to great force of breath. In fact, the breathy quality of Caruso's late recordings was largely due to his declining vocal mechanism and efforts to compensate. The unhappy truth is that driving the voice by "breath congestion", as it is called, is a practice guaranteed to produce vocal short-gevity. (Husler and Rodd-Marling, 1976, pp. 129-132) E. H. Gombrich writing about the visual arts cites the power of representational precedent to overcome direct observation in the drawing of rhinoceri in the late Middle Ages. Originally depicted by Dürer in 1515 as having armor plates, rhinoceri continued long thereafter to be represented with plates even when drawn "from life". (Gombrich, 1965, pp. 81-82)

Tradition is of course equally adept at perpetuating intellectual errors in textbooks and histories such as the apocryphal story of Galileo hefting cannon balls to the top of the leaning tower of Pisa to test his theories (Koyré, 1937, pp. 441-453; cited in Scheffler, 1965, p. 49) or the persistent notion, rehearsed in countless elementary science texts, that induction proceeds from the particular to the general while deduction does the reverse. (Skyrms, 1966, pp. 13-15) In these and similar ways, practising and traditional practices may fall far short of perfection.

The Social Images of Practice

Imagination plays an important role not only in practising but in how we think about practice—what I shall call the "social images" of practice. Not all of them are salutary, as witness this Elizabethan limerick.

> Multiplication is vexation,
> Division is as bad;
> The Rule of Three doth puzzle me,
> And Practice drives me mad.
>   (Anonymous MS dated 1570)

I have already mentioned the popular notion of practising as bovine persistence in the face of drudgery—the idea that mere repetition is sufficient, eventually, to "get it right" and to be able to "do it without thinking".[3] While I deny that the repetition is either "mere" or sufficient for the purposes mentioned, there is a psychological truth contained in this portrait. Ironically, it has to do with the pleasures of repetition.

As one achieves a level of proficiency at various skills—for example, basic carpentry, running scales, volleying in tennis, or swimming, a rhythmic ease of performance and a sensation of felt fluency gradually pervades the activity. One becomes smoothly coordinated, absorbed, and focussed *through* the repetitions in an almost trance-like way. Something of a balance between outgoing effort and undergoing results is achieved that is pleasing in itself. Dewey describes this sort of "integral experience" as the opposite of arrest or stasis, as a kind of "reconstruction" of experience (Dewey, 1934, 1958, p. 41) and indeed it is. For the reconstruction is of one's own abilities and of the sometimes painful and frustrating sensations of their exercise.

The satisfying resolution of such struggles in a fluid performance is part of the rhythmic joy of practise and in large part accounts for one's ability to keep at it. The pay off—the motivation to go on—is at least as much in the internal, *felt* balance of effort and achievement as in the achievement itself.[4] This is the "aesthetic face" of learning by instruction and practise, yet another manifestation of that education of the sensibilities so valued by Schiller and later to influence heavily Dewey's theory of experience. (Dewey, 1934, Chapter 3, *passim*)

Besides the idea of practising as repetitious drudgery, the notion of *a* (the) practice may carry with it a social image, perhaps several conflicting or contrasting images, of what that practice is or ought to be. Rightly *and* wrongly, narrowly *and* broadly, certain preconceptions attach themselves to what it is to practice law or medicine, to be a musician, to be a violinist, even to play in a certain manner or style. "Schools" of training and instruction in painting, music, architecture, science, business, and the like, promote quite different conceptions of the "done thing", of what is customary in the way of *the* practices to be acquired and mastered.

In classical voice studies, for instance, one quickly absorbs the different sound and performance ideals of the "German" and "Italian" schools including their respective repertoires. Even individual voices are cast into evocative categories: the slightly reedy quality of the "Irish" tenors such as John MacCormick or Robert White; the full throated sounds of the "Italian" traditionalists Renata Tibaldi or Luciano Pavarotti; the large, four-square sound of the "German" Helden singers Birget Nilsson and Lauritz Melchior; the mellifluous richness of the Lieder singers Dietrich Fischer-Dieskau and Janet Baker; the silvery sheen of the "Scandinavian" school manifested in the vocal qualities of Jussi Bjoerling or Nicolai Gedda. However vague, overlapping, and rooted in temperamental and linguistic differences, in local music culture and composition, in the fame of individual singers, or in historical accident, such vagrant social imagery significantly influences the very ideas and ideals of singing—what it is, what it involves, and what it aspires to.

Similar variations in social imagery of the done thing shape the practices of many fields and occupations. Michael Polanyi, for example, notes the atavistic power of certain places and institutions to promote an atmosphere of scientific apprenticeship. "The regions of Europe in which the scientific method first originated 400 years ago are scientifically still more fruitful today, in spite of their impoverishment, than several overseas areas where much more money is available for scientific research." (Polanyi, 1958, p. 53) Of course, times and traditions change, migrate (often through immigration of a few "masters"), and get born anew in response to new demands—as witness the achievements in atomic science of the Manhattan project during WW II, or the peculiar mystique in the second half of the twentieth century of the Harvard Business School in American commerce, or the IBM "corporate image" right down to sartorial style and comportment.

The fact that some of the social imagery of certain fields or occupations may turn out on closer inspection to be utter nonsense or prejudicial is quite beside the point. Whether or not deserved, accurate, or inspiring, such social imagery in the arts, sciences and professions comprises a fabric of suggestion and preconception of varying regulative force. For good or ill (and probably both) social imagery helps to shape and direct the practices within a given field: how they are seen, how they are done, and how they are taught.

The conceptual point is this: even as practising may exceed in accomplishment the limits of established practice *the* practice is a far broader concept than practising. To take a musical example: how one plays the cello depends not only upon one's daily practise regimen. It depends also upon the particular tradition of cello instruction into which one is initiated; upon the place of the cello in the orchestra; upon the performance history and tradition of the instrument and its virtuosi; upon the available repertoire and acoustical properties of the instrument; even upon the physical image and posture of the player. Before the novice ever gets to a teacher, he or she is beset by all sorts of preconceptions, many of them destined to be undone, no doubt, that society reinforces willy nilly. This aura of preconception constitutes the *social practice* of cello playing, not to be confused with the many episodes of cello practicing under the tutelage of an instructor. A condition of learning any advanced skill[5] is initiation into *the* practices of that skill *as seen from the inside*; usually by an instructor who, if not now or ever an advanced practitioner, nonetheless understands those practices from the standpoint of how they may be learned, practised, and performed. That is as much a matter of learning by example as by precept and practise.

Practice and the Imagination

Teaching, like other service professions—law, psychiatry, medicine, religion—has its share of quacks and charlatans for whom *the* practice is their practice, *the* way *their* way, usually garnished with guarantees of success. Caught between unquestioning faith in "the method" and following orders, the TIPS formula therewith drops to its lowest common denominator: indoctrination. In fact, however, the practice of teaching, again like the practices of psychiatry or law, comprises many subpractices some of them conflicting, some reliable, some questionable.

In *Artistry*, for instance, I described the predicament of the fledgling singer confronted by the plethora of theories and therapies, techniques, precepts, and exercises for training the voice.

" . . . the various accounts of the voice and advice proffered present a bewildering (and depressing) spectacle of conflicting opinion—for instance, that voices are born and not made; that though born, they can at least be made over; that one should sing as little children scream, or as an adult whispers, or as a dog yawns; that a refined 'technique' is the singer's salvation; that one should dispense with all technique and sing 'naturally'; that speech and singing are the same and should be developed coordinately or one 'from' the other; that the two are entirely different and must be developed separately; that the singer must 'drive' the voice by a great effort of muscle and breath; that singing should be totally effortless and free of all tension. Simultaneously, the voices of great singers are often invoked to 'prove' the wisdom of this or that way of singing." (Howard, 1982, p. 33)

Analogues of this cacophony pervade nearly every domain of instruction but particularly those where the subject matter, if laudable enough, is also ineffable: "creativity skills", "critical thinking skills", "leadership skills", "business success skills", and the like. Where the ingredients of competent practice are so vague, the way is open for quick-fix gurus of every stripe to take advantage of the unwary, the ambitious, and the desperate. (Cf. Lindsey, article in *New York Times*, 29 September 1986)

How can we protect ourselves against foolishness? A marked feature of foolishness, aside from its ubiquity, is its *total* indifference to truth and falsity, unlike lying, for instance, which pays at least covert respect to truth. (Frankfurt, 1986, p. 90) At the very least this suggests that unfettered imagination *could* be a dangerous thing in professional training seriously undermining the very quest for mastery it supposedly drives.

For the practically minded among theorists such risk is enough to cast general suspicion on imaginations's freer flights. Dewey, for one, sharply distinguishes the "imaginative" from the "imaginary", the "imagination" from "pure fancy". (Dewey, 1934, pp. 267-269) Imagination or what we call the imaginative remain "embodied" in reality, he maintains, transforming it in at first unfamiliar but enduring ways. Whereas, the imaginary is "arbitrary" forming "the matter of reverie, of dream; ideas are floating, not anchored to any existence as its property, its possession of meanings. Emotions that are equally loose and floating cling to these ideas. The pleasure they afford is the reason why they are entertained and are allowed to occupy the scene; they are attached to existence only in a way that, as long as sanity abides, is felt to be only fanciful and unreal." (1934, p. 273)

Earlier on in his career Dewey similarly wagged a warning finger at the unfettered imagination and its specious emotional satisfactions. "Except where there is a disciplined disposition, the tendency is for the imagination to run loose. Instead of its objects being checked up by conditions with reference to their practicability in execution, they are allowed to develop because of the immediate emotional satisfaction which they yield." (Dewey, 1916, p. 348)

This suspicion of naughty imagination lost in day dreams connects to Dewey's basic concern throughout his *corpus* to keep thinking in general (which he views as highly imaginative) and theory in particular closely connected to action and reality; but I am less concerned with exegesis than with how imagination affects and is affected by established practice.

It comes as no surprise that the some of the practices of a given field may themselves be as "fanciful" (baseless, misleading, mistaken) as the wildest products of fiction, as witness the host of theories and regimens of vocal training aforementioned. Or, to take an intellectual skill, consider the long standing practice of justifying the study of formal logic as producing generally better "critical thinkers". (Cf. McPeck, 1981, pp. 25-26) The "reality" into which we get initiated by instruction and established practices may itself turn out to be pure fancy in the degenerate sense of chicanery. Conversely, the "done thing", even where demonstrated reliable or effective for certain purposes, may severely hobble imagination depending upon how *the* practice is presented to us: as an aid to development, as a way, or as the one and only way to go.

For these reasons, I cannot agree that the differences between the imaginary and the imaginative are quite so pat as Dewey makes them appear; or, that there is no place for pure fancy in the assessment of established practices whether of an intellectual or physically procedural sort. It is a question always of what shall count as a "realistic" use of imagination, and that can vary mightily with time, chance, and discovery. It may in fact require an exercise of pure fancy (even if it turns out to be nonsense) to escape the bonds and limitations of established practice or to break onto new ground.

Let us see how this might work out in an actual case. The example is John Passmore's. He suggests that the historical topic of when and where Columbus landed in America can be taught "in a way which raises questions about what would have happened had he landed elsewhere in America, or at a somewhat different time, or under different national auspices." (Passmore, 1980, p. 149) He goes on to say, following Dewey, that to contemplate the *"purely* imaginary—what is not, in my phrase, a 'real alternative'—is not thus fruitful"; for example, that Columbus "arrived in America by jet-plane". (pp. 149-150) This is not a real alternative, he says, because "the entire historical situation would have had to be different in almost every respect.   By imagining this to have happened, therefore, we throw no light on the actual situation." (p. 150) Like Dewey, Passmore raises the spectre of naughty imagination on the loose: "The purest form of fancy is a day-dream. A day-dream toys with possibilities which are not 'real alternatives'; its sole function is an escape from reality, it is not a path to problem-solving, understanding, creating." (p. 151)

As a blanket statement, this carries the notion of what is not a real alternative in speculation, theory, or in fact rather too far. There are day-dreams and there are day-dreams, some suggesting heretofore unthinkable possibilities. What if Columbus *had* arrived in America by jet-plane? Might he not have triggered off the beginnings of another "cargo cult" comparable to the one among the natives of New Zealand? Wouldn't America have had to be an exceedingly isolated and primitive place in an otherwise advanced industrial world? What could possibly have brought about that state of affairs? Could some parts of the world have reached twentieth-century levels of science and technology by the end of the fifteenth century? My point is that these questions are not *altogether* foolish, and even if they have little to do with Columbus' actual voyage and landing, they do evoke other "real alternatives" to past or present events, and they do stimulate thinking in ways that might reasonably be considered as in the interest of problem-solving, understanding, and creating.[6]

If fanciful imagination is often needed to break through extant practice or tradition, imaginal controls of the sort earlier discussed are also needed to sustain the activity of practising. For the learner of advanced skills, salvation is to be found neither in unfettered fancy, nor in the done thing, but in the interaction between them. For that, it takes as much imagination to be initiated *into* the practices of a given field or discipline as it does to overcome the fetters of past precedent.

For the learner of advanced skills, salvation is to be found neither in unfettered fancy nor in the done thing but in the interaction between them. For that, it takes as much imagination to be initiated into the practices of a given field or discipline as it does to overcome the fetters of past precedent.

The Ambiguity of Practice

What is routine and what is intelligent about practice? How do means and ends get connected up in ways that enable us to improve? To answer those questions, we need to consider both sides of the concept of practice. If by practice we mean learning by repeated trial or performance, the concept is ambiguous as between drill and training. Certain habits, routines, and basic facilities like learning the alphabet or multiplication table are built up by drill to the point where, as Ryle says, one can "do them in his sleep". (Ryle, 1949/1984, pp. 42-43) "Training, on the other hand, though it embodies plenty of sheer drill, does not consist of drill. It involves the stimulation by criticism and example of the pupil's own judgement. He learns how to do things thinking what he is doing, so that every operation is itself a new lesson to him how to perform better"— what Ryle calls "intelligent capacities". He concludes, "Drill dispenses with intelligence, training develops it. We do not expect the soldier to be able to read maps 'in his sleep'". (p. 43)

Scheffler also notes the critical importance for education of the ambiguity of practise as between those situations where "unthinking repetition is the rule" and those where "opportunities for engaging the student's judgement" come into play. (Scheffler, 1965, p. 103) For one, "*Practice* [practise] in professional education is thus misconceived if assimilated to the model of drill or to the repeated study of standard cases". And for another, implied by " . . . the emphasis on *critical* practice is that performance and intelligence do not belong in strictly separated compartments"—the former thought to be "routine and habitual" and the latter "spontaneous and innovative". (p. 103)

I quite agree with both writers except for Ryle's tag line that drill dispenses with intelligence while training develops it. Being able to do something "in one's sleep" or "without thinking about it" is an *achievement* often the result of considerable exercise of intelligence on the part of the learner and careful intervention by an instructor. One is required to hold specific ends-in-view through trial after trial until errors become recognized as such and are eliminated. If routine response is the outcome, such response hardly "dispenses with intelligence" in the making. In learning to play harmonic drills at the piano, for example, one must initially think where to place the fingers on the keyboard while reading the score.

Training, in the sense of critical practise, aims to develop critical *skills* (Ryle's "intelligent capacities") requiring the exercise of judgement and choice both in their making and in their deployment. Yet one cannot relegate all routine to the activity or the results of drill. As I have argued elsewhere, an essential feature of critical skills is

> ". . . their irreducibility *overall* to routine response. Unlike, for example, a simple tracking task in a psychological experiment, a critical skill involves continuous, judgement-based adjustment of responses . . . to changing contingencies. Judgements, like anything else, may fall into standard patterns, and to that degree they admit of partial routinization. They may even admit of algorithmic representation as do the elementary valid argument forms in logic. But new contingencies will always arise to challenge the performer of complex tasks." (Howard, 1982, p. 182)

So, it is no contradiction to think of Boris Spatsky making certain highly complex (but routine to him) moves in chess "without thinking" or of Frederika von Stade day-dreaming of pizza during a "routine" opera performance. [7]

To sum up: even as training is irreducible to routine response, neither is drill, notwithstanding the latter's *achievement* of routine response; neither is routine response entirely absent from the achievements of training in exercising critical skills of performance. Intelligence *and* routine are to be found at both ends of the practise spectrum—in drill and in training—despite their different emphases and outcomes. [8]

Practising and Routine

Recall now the familiar portrait of drill as the slowest, if surest, common denominator of the TIPS formula. The thoughtless routine of drill nonetheless requires discipline and direction; it isn't easy because it's drudgery. Accordingly, practise requires a regimen: a set of precise exercises directed at specific ends *and* the authority of an instructor both to see that they get done and done well. Eventually, talent—if it is sufficient—and training—if it is rigorous enough—will win out over tedium. If not, then the potential was never there in the first place.

This picture of practise, particularly of drill, though not uncommon, contains a number of questionable assumptions, half truths, and plain falsehoods. Most glaring is the assumption that talent is a given, something fixed by nature and awaiting the molding process of proper instruction and diligent practise. Suffice it to say that whatever is "given" by nature is highly volatile and changeable with time, training, and opportunity. Talent and potential, rather than explaining eventual success or failure, themselves require to be explained; they tend in any event to be estimated by circular reference to how well one performs en route. In effect, appeals to vague notions of talent, gifts, or potential are more like excuses or praise than explanation.

Besides fixed potential, another difficulty with the TIPS formula is its reliance upon a "static" technology of fixed means to fixed ends. As Dewey reminds us, we tend rather to learn advanced skills within a *continuum* of means-ends in which the latter are mutually revisible. (Dewey, 1939/1972, pp. 40-50) That is, as our competence increases we alter not only what we do but also our conceptions of what we are doing and trying to achieve.[9] The very same exercise, for example, can have several different objectives which, as we realise them, are then seen as related to others as one facility embeds within another.

Consider, for example, what is involved in running scales on the piano. The same series of notes is repeated over and over: now for pitch accuracy, now for phraseology, now for dynamics, now for dexterity at increasing tempi, and so on. One always has an end-in-view, a particular achievement in mind, for which the exercise is being repeated. Each trial represents a *different* successive approximation to that end-in-view. The larger goal of course is to gain control of all these variables at once.

The connection of means to ends in drill, still more in training, is similarly misrepresented in the TIPS formula by mechanical-causal analogy, as if the running off of routines *automatically* achieved their ends. On this view, the only deficits possible are in the amounts of talent and tenacity required to achieve the specified result. One fails either because one "just doesn't have it" (lacked intelligence) or because one "didn't try hard enough" (lacked diligence). This view obscures the roles of intelligence, choice, and imagination in practice: intelligence in the form of growing discrimination through trial and error; choice in the form of decisions about what corrections to make; and imagination in the form of imaginal controls (like metaphor and analogy) and holding ends-in-view.

Drill as Thoughtful Action

Whatever else may be said about drill, it is an action, not something that "happens" to us. Writing about action in general, Scheffler remarks as follows on its "time-binding" character. "It should not be thought mysterious that the scene of human action . . . runs both backward and forward from the immediate present. For all action links past and future, organizing or 'binding' time in a characteristic way. Performed with a certain outcome in view and with further consequences anticipated, an action starts out with implicit reference to the future. But it also involves an estimate of prevailing conditions in virtue of which the action to be performed is deemed to have a good chance of succeeding. And such judgement itself, whether sound or not, purports to find its basis in past trials or past testimony." (Scheffler, 1985, p. 22)

As a species of action, practise—both drill and training—is similarly time-binding of past and future within a specious present.[10] That is, trial and error learning involves a compound of memory and anticipation in which imagination's job is to hold future ends *in view* and the past *in review* even as we prepare to take the next step. Only thus can we monitor our own progress and learn from our mistakes. And only thus can we make sense of how the rules and routines of practise connect means to ends.

As I put it elsewhere, "Until they are enacted, how are means and ends-in-view *held*? With the possible exceptions of recipes and drill manuals, they are not simply read off from either tradition or the particular situation confronting one. Rather . . . they are held in imagination as directives (rules and routines) and frequently revised therein according to the exigences of the situation. In effect, it is imagination that enables us to adjust our know-how to particular cases and even to revise it or transfer it to new realms of application." (Howard, 1982, p. 135)

Finally, the TIPS formula for practise entirely ignores the subtle relations among tradition, demonstration, and learning. In acquiring a practice, we also practise to learn it. We strive to perform it in ritualistic fashion. Put to the test, it soon becomes public what we do or do not know, can or cannot do. This sounds like worship; but not only in religious ritual is performance of the rite a demonstration that serves to pass it on to others. (Cf. Scheffler, 1986, Ch. 6) The rituals of art, science, technology, and education have a similar function. Practising their rituals simultaneously exemplifies *the* practices of those fields and becomes a way for others to learn them—and to surpass them.

Accordingly, we may distinguish the cross-sectional, "synchronic" instructional pay off of practising particular facilities from the longitudinal, "diachronic" pay off of traditional practices. The latter teach across historical time, as it were, from one generation to the next. The former is more a matter of identifying *with* the practices of a given field or discipline, of taking them into oneself, of mastering them for the sake of competency. That is very like a process of initiation into a tradition by aspiration, demonstration, and precept.

We cannot escape the traditional demands of our chosen disciplines or professions however much we may eventually depart from them. We grow into them precisely in order to grow beyond them and maybe alter them for future generations. Yet none of this personal and historical drama of learning is captured in the simplistic notion of drill as drudgery (nor in the equally simplistic assimilation of training to drill). Drill, on the contrary, is one of the most powerful, intelligent, imaginative means of learning at our disposal enabling us to master the facilities required by advanced skills. Through drill we not only learn by example and instruction, but become examples of the very things we learn. One might even think of this as the existential predicament of practising anything at all: you are what you learn to do routinely.

Notes

1 Many doctoral theses and research proposals in education fall into this general pattern, not only in curriculum studies but in leadership, management, and policy studies as well. The tendency to a reductive, pseudo-empiricism is further exacerbated by the "request for proposal" documents emanating from private and government funding agencies. Whether researchers are pandering to agency preconceptions or the reverse is a chicken-and-egg question I happily bequeath to sociologists of knowledge.

2 On the varieties and "myths" of potential in educational thought see Israel Scheffler's *Of Human Potential* (1985). See also Chapter 5, "Knowledge and Skill" of his *Conditions of Knowledge* (1965) and Chapter 6, "Practice and the Vision of Mastery" in my *Artistry* (1982). The latter two especially undergird much of the present discussion.

3 In *Artistry* (1982, p. 158), I called this the Penelope Theory of practise so named after Penelope, the weaving wife of Odysseus.

4 Here, as elsewhere, e.g., feeling that one "knows", the sensations alone of fluency and security are no reliable guide to the worth of the actual achievement.

5 Here I am using the phrase 'advanced skill' as roughly synonymous with 'field', 'discipline', or 'art form' which typically require the mastery of many subskills or facilities. For a discussion of the conceptual ranges and relations of skills, facilities ("techniques"), and habits, see *Artistry*, pp. 176-185.

6 And as the history of science-fiction writing from Verne to Azamov amply shows, yesterday's fancy may well become today's or tomorrow's real alternative.

7 I recall her making this remark during an entre-act radio interview, but I cannot recall when or the performance except that it was opera. "What were you thinking of during the second act?" was the question. "Pizza!" came the reply.

8 In this connection, see Passmore on "open" and "closed" capacities. "A 'closed' capacity is distinguishable from an 'open' capacity in virtue of the fact that it allows of total mastery [by practise—presumably drill].

Take, for example, the capacity to count." One speaks of "learning the secret" of games like naughts and crosses; but, Passmore says, "In the case of an open capacity there is no secret to be learned. One cannot 'learn the secret' of writing poetry or of doing philosophy." (1980, pp. 40-41) It is precisely such futile quest to "learn the secret" that promotes the "bag of tricks" approach in public education and professional training to open capacities like critical thinking, creativity, and decision making.

9 Dewey's notion of a continuum of ends-means applies as much to the *learning* of so-called "closed capacities" like typing or spelling (eventually to become routine) as to the mature exercise of "open capacities" like chess or musical performance. See footnote 8 above.

10 "Specious" in the sense of a present that is ever changing, of varying "width", as it were, and not literally a point psychologically in time or consciousness.

References

Jerome S. Bruner, *Actual Minds, Possible Worlds* (Cambridge: Harvard University Press, 1986).

John Dewey, *Democracy and Education* (New York: Macmillan, 1966); first published in 1916.

John Dewey, *Art as Experience*, (New York: Putnam, 1958); first published in 1934.

John Dewey, *Theory of Valuation* (Chicago: University of Chicago Press, 1972); first published in 1939.

Harry Frankfurt, "On Bullshit", *Raritan*, vol. 1, no. 2, Fall 1986, pp. 81-100.

E. H. Gombrich, *Art and Illusion*, 2nd ed. (New York: Random House, 1965).

V. A. Howard, *Artistry, The Work of Artists* (Indianapolis: Hackett, 1982).

Frederick Husler and Yvonne Rodd-Marling, *Singing, The Physical Nature of the Vocal Organ* (London: Hutchinson, 1976).

Arthur R. Jensen, *Straight Talk About Mental Tests* (New York: Free Press, 1981).

Arthur R. Jensen, *Genetics and Education* (London: Methuen, 1972).

Jerome Kagan and Orville G. Brim Jr., eds., *Constancy and Change in Human Development* (Cambridge: Harvard University Press, 1980).

A. Koyré, "Galilée et l'Expérience de Pise", *Annales de l'Université de Paris* (1937), pp. 441-453.

Robert Lindsey, "Spiritual Concepts Drawing a Different Breed of Adherent", *New York Times*, 29 September 1986.

John E. McPeck, *Critical Thinking and Education* (New York: St. Martin's Press, 1981).

John Passmore, *The Philosophy of Teaching* (Cambridge: Harvard University Press, 1980).

Gilbert Ryle, *The Concept of Mind* (Chicago: University of Chicago Press, 1984); first published in 1949.

Carl E. Seashore, *In Search of Beauty in Music, A Scientific Approach to Musical Esthetics* (New York: The Ronald Press, 1947).

Israel Scheffler, *Inquiries, Philosophical Studies of Language, Science, and Learning* (Indianapolis: Hackett, 1986).

Israel Scheffler, *Of Human Potential* (London: Routledge & Kegan Paul, 1985).

Israel Scheffler, *The Conditions of Knowledge* (Glenview: Scott, Foresman, 1965; reprinted by the University of Chicago Press, 1985).

B. F. Skinner, *Science and Human Behaviour* (New York: Free Press, 1965).

Brian Skyrms, *Choice and Chance, An Introduction to Inductive Logic* (Belmont: Dickenson, 1966).

7

Learning by Example

According to me, all writing is and should be to some extent a process of imitation; you like reading, you read a lot in general, you find yourself attracted to a particular kind of subdivision of literature, you read that kind intensively, you reach a stage where you begin to think perhaps you can contribute something of that kind yourself. That is probably what is meant by a tradition; it was certainly what got me started on writing in the distant past.

—Kingsley Amis

On Being an Example

The range of learning by example far exceeds that of formal instruction, training, or practice crossing boundaries of time and tradition and even conscious intention. Moreover, examples may be given and taken, given but not taken, taken but not given, living or dead; and, of course, they may be verbal or nonverbal, understood or misunderstood whether good or bad.

To begin with a deceptively simple question: What is it to be an example? What, for instance, distinguishes "showing" from "telling", on the one hand, and demonstrating something from just doing it, on the other? A first response might be that telling is a verbal, symbolic activity, whereas showing and demonstrating, are nonverbal, nonsymbolic activities. Another might be that the difference between doing and demonstrating is that the latter "speaks for itself" with instructional intent, whereas the former, lacking instructional intent, doesn't bother.

As with common sense theories of instruction and practice, this conception of what it is to be an example is less sense than common. It errs not only in assuming that the verbal and the nonverbal correspond to the symbolic and the nonsymbolic but in further assuming those differences to correspond to the difference between telling and showing. This conception of an example errs again in appealing to "instructional intent" to explain example status when, if anything, the latter is more likely to explain the former. And finally, nonverbal "speaking for itself" is either an inappropriate metaphor or a flat contradiction. This all deserves some spelling out.

First of all, showing and telling do not correspond to the difference between the nonverbal and the verbal, because as much "showing" is verbal as nonverbal. Likewise a good deal of the "telling" takes the form of nonverbal instruction as previously discussed. Even if "telling" is restricted to verbal instructions, the correspondence does not hold up generally because so many illustrations, demonstrations, and examples take verbal form. Virtually everywhere, showing and telling cut across the difference between verbal and nonverbal versions of things.

Second, the verbal-nonverbal dichotomy is itself misleading, being ambiguous in its distinction between verbal and nonverbal tokens of *language* (e.g., spoken and written words) and linguistic and *nonlinguistic* symbol systems (e.g., language and pictures). The former distinction is no help in salvaging the presumed difference between showing and telling, since examples do not always take written form, obviously. But neither is the latter distinction much help for the opposite reason that many examples *do* take linguistic form spoken and written. So on either construal of the verbal-nonverbal dichotomy, we are no further ahead.

Third, neither construal just mentioned of the verbal-nonverbal dichotomy corresponds to the difference between the symbolic and the nonsymbolic. To stop talking and resort instead to a picture or diagram is not to leave the realm of the symbolic; it is rather to shift from one symbolic system to another. Still, it might be argued that some examples are nonsymbolic in the sense of being instances of physical actions or behaviour. But how then to distinguish an instance from an example? Surely an example of a triangle, a physical action or other behaviour is an instance of it, but not always conversely. To be an example of this or that requires something more than being just an instance of it. Not every occurrence of vermillion in the world is a sample of vermillion, an example of the colour, even if any one taken at random *could* take on that function. But that is the very point: what is it to take on that function, to be an example of vermillion and not just another instance?

Perhaps "instructional intent" will come to the rescue. An instance, it might be said, becomes an example (and, incidentally, able to "speak for itself") when it is used with instructional intent, otherwise not. But here we come full circle once again to the question, what is it for an instance to be so *used?*

Since we are left with the same question we began with, we have no choice but to start over, this time without the impediments of nonverbal, nonsymbolic examples that speak for themselves.

On Being an Example II

I shall argue that the shift from "telling" to "showing" is no more of an exit from the realm of the symbolic than would be the shift from a description to a diagram. While the shift from telling to showing may be from a linguistic to a nonlinguistic symbol system, that is not always so, and the most fundamental shift is in the *direction* of the reference involved. That change of direction in the way that symbols refer is one that Goodman calls "exemplification". In ordinary speech the word 'example' is often used as a synonym of 'instance'. To eliminate the ambiguity, I shall adopt a technical usage of 'example' to indicate something that refers by exemplification. (Goodman, 1972, pp. 50-52) As a central, technical concept in Goodmanian symbol theory, exemplification requires only summary presentation here as it bears upon the nature of "showing" and what it means to be an example.

Goodman's favourite example of an example is a sample of cloth—a tailor's swatch. (Goodman, 1972, p. 53ff; 1978, p. 63ff) Let us say that it is a sample of navy herringbone weave. Now to be a sample of navy herringbone weave, the labels 'navy' and 'herringbone weave' must properly apply to the swatch. That is, the swatch must possess those properties among others; otherwise it may be a sample of something else but certainly not of navy herringbone weave.[1] To be a sample, however, and not merely an instance, the swatch must also refer *back* to those properties by "exhibiting" them, "showing them forth", as we say.

How does that come about? In logical terminology, if we think of the predicates, 'navy' and 'herringbone weave' as denoting the swatch, the reference of the swatch itself "runs . . . in the opposite direction—runs up from rather than down to what is denoted." (Goodman, 1972, p. 52) In other words, the swatch refers back to the predicates that denote it. That is why Goodman describes exemplification as "possession plus reference . . . The swatch exemplifies only those properties it both has and refers to." (p. 53) More precisely stated, "Exemplification is restricted only insofar as the denotation of the label in question is regarded as having been antecedently fixed." (p. 59)

Of course, the swatch has other properties too such as its size, shape, weight, date of manufacture, and the like, which it does not normally exemplify. Which ones it does exemplify, "depends upon what particular system of symbolization is in effect" (p. 53), that is to say, which *selection* of properties is relevant in the circumstances. "The tailor's sample does not normally function as a sample of a tailor's sample; it normally exemplifies certain properties of a material, but not the property of exemplifying such properties. Yet if offered in response to a question about what a tailor's sample is, the swatch may indeed exemplify the property of being a tailor's sample". (pp. 53-54) Which is to say that another selection from among the swatch's possessed properties would have been made.

That same selective feature of sampling also allows for something other than a tailor's swatch to serve as a sample of navy herringbone weave, say, the sleeve of my suit which does not normally have that function. Even as samples select from among their various properties certain ones for "showing", so also we may select our samples from any instance of navy herringbone weave to show what it is. While some things such as swatches are typically *samples* (i.e., normally have that function) other typical *instances* such as sleeves may momentarily serve that function. As a referential function, exemplification like other symbol functions may come and go.[2] Consequently, we are not bound to using only "official" tailor's swatches; we may select at convenience any piece of navy herringbone weave to represent the whole. So once we learn what to look for in the sample, the world of navy herringbone weave opens up to us. That simple fact of exemplificational reference has important pedagogical consequences for how we learn from the world at large as we shall see later on.

For now, we may say this much: that to be an example of any kind—sample, illustration, demonstration, exemplar—is to be an exemplifier within a symbolic nexus with all the logical restrictions and cognitive opportunities that implies. And as for the difference between doing and demonstrating something, it is sufficient for the doing to be an instance of something that it be properly labelled, that it possess the properties ascribed to it. For that same doing to become a demonstration, however, requires that it refer back to those labelled properties—that *it* refer exemplificationally besides being referred *to* denotationally—that it become an exhibit as well as an action of a particular kind, a "showing" as well as a "doing". (Cf. Howard, 1982, pp. 100-101)

The Continuum of Show and Tell

Commenting on instruction by demonstration, Goodman says,

> "The gymnastics instructor, unlike the orchestra conductor, gives samples. His demonstrations exemplify the requisite properties of the actions to be performed by his class, whereas his oral instructions prescribe rather than show what is to be done. The proper response to his knee-bend is a knee-bend; the proper response to his shout 'lower' is not to shout 'lower' but to bend deeper. Nevertheless, since the demonstrations are part of the instruction, are accompanied by and may be replaced by verbal directions, and have no already established denotation, they may—like any sample not otherwise committed as to denotation—also be taken as denoting what the predicates they exemplify denote, and are then labels[3] exemplifying themselves." (Goodman, 1972, p. 63)

In the passage just quoted, one of a series exploring the relations between "samples and labels", Goodman stumbles onto a fundamental insight into show and tell pedagogy; namely, that showing and telling are intersecting functions, arranged on a continuum rather than always conjunctive, talk-and-do instruction. Otherwise put, the "shift" involved in switching from telling to showing may be twofold: in the direction of the reference: from denotation to exemplification; but also in the labels themselves: from verbal descriptions and directives exemplified by sample actions to actions that are self-referential. (Cf Howard, 1972, p. 101) We might have suspected as much from the fact, noted earlier, that not all "telling" is explicitly verbal (linguistic) any more than all "showing" is nonverbal. [4]

What happens at the intersection, where showing and telling converge? Consider Goodman's example above. The student gymnast's knee-bend is clearly an action in response to instruction, an *instance* of a knee-bend. The instructor's knee-bend is just as clearly a demonstration (an exemplifying instance). But, "since the demonstrations are part of the instruction, *are accompanied by and may be replaced by verbal directions*" (italics mine), the instructor's knee-bend becomes self-referential in the sense of denoting all knee-bends (including itself) that exemplify a proper knee-bend. In other words, at one referential extreme is the verbal directive, "lower", and at the other, the nonverbal, demonstration knee-bend in the typical talk-and-do situation. Gradually, however, as the student gymnast's grasp of the proper motion improves, the instructor will often dispense with verbal directives in favour of knee-bends that both direct and demonstrate simultaneously. The effect is rather like playing an accordion, compressing directives and demonstrations together from opposite directions into directive demonstrations.

That, if we are to make any sense of the phrase at all, is what is meant by saying that such demonstrations "speak for themselves": they do so by dropping all the talk that led up to the point where the instructor's knee-bend becomes a label exemplifying itself. The instructor's literally speaking is replaced by the metaphoric "speaking for itself" of his demonstration. The latter shows more than can or ever need be told. [5]

This is a common enough occurrence, but it requires a convergence of attention by instructor and learner on the relevant details in order for the demonstration to "speak for itself". Up to then, a good deal of talk may be required to put the learner in the way of those details. Ryle makes a similar observation in his remarks on the competency of one person to judge the performance of another. "If I am competent to judge your performance, then in witnessing it I am on the alert to detect mistakes and muddles in it, but so are you in executing it; I am ready to notice advantages you might take of pieces of luck, but so are you. You learn as you proceed, and I too learn as you proceed. The intelligent performer operates critically, the intelligent spectator follows critically. Roughly, execution and understanding are merely different exercises of knowledge of tricks of the same trade." (Ryle, 1949, p. 55)

Now Ryle is mainly concerned here with what is involved in intelligently "following" (i.e., understanding) what another person is doing. While "following" and execution can be separated as in spectator sports, sitting in the audience, appreciating art, or in "criticism" of various kinds, they converge in countless learning situations where the doing is itself a kind of "following" on the part of the learner and a form of criticism on the part of the instructor. If, as luck and persistence would have it, one reaches a stage where a single demonstration is worth a thousand words, it is only because it is clear in principle what such thousand words would be about. (See Howard, 1982, p. 100)

Becoming an "intelligent follower" in Ryle's sense of the phrase may be seen as a necessary condition of autonomy in learning by example, a matter of knowing what to look for, not only in the examples presented in formal instruction, but in those we discover for ourselves. How we scour the world for examples to learn from is the subject of the rest of this chapter. To understand that quest, we first need to examine how different instructional demands shape the most common ways of showing.

Some Varieties of Showing

Showing, no less than telling, is polychromatic. It is not one thing but many. Its composition depends upon the symbol systems in force, the instructional demands of subject matter and of learners themselves. From ritual reenactments to flight simulators, from model ships to mathematical models, from tailors' swatches to open lessons, the landscape of learning by examples presents a staggering variety.

As a first cut at sorting the conceptual geography of that landscape, I propose a few rough categories of examples, by no means exhaustive, based less upon their symbolic types than upon their instructional purposes. As I have been doing throughout, I will reserve the term 'example' to refer generally to the whole range of exemplifiers from which we may learn and 'showing' to those that are associated with instruction(s) as discussed in Chapter 5. As with the rest of the categories proposed, that becomes a fine line to draw as we approach self-instruction. However, the aim is not to define away entrenched ambiguities in what, after all, are everyday concepts but to provide insight into our customary ways of showing and of being shown.

Among the ways of showing by examples that stand out in instructional experience are four: first, is that of a *sample* or typical (exemplifying) instance; second, is that of a *model* in the sense of a scaled up or scaled down design of structure, pattern, or function; third, is that of a *simulation* which approximates in varying ways and degrees to the real thing; and fourth is that of an *exemplar* taken to be a perfect replica or "ideal" realisation.[6] As found, these are hardly distinct, unambiguous notions, since a sample of gold or navy herringbone weave could well be exemplary, and one use of the word 'model' as in 'model student' is synonymous with being an ideal or exemplary student. And a flight simulator is sometimes described as a "mock up" or full scale model of a cockpit. Still, slippery as they are, samples, models, simulations, and exemplars represent different ways exemplification may function in response to instructional requirements.

The signal for a sample or typical exemplifying instance is usually a request or prefatory statement to the effect, "Could you give a demonstration (an illustration, an example) of . . . ", "For example . . . ", "For instance . . . " "To illustrate . . . ", "To demonstrate . . . " We may ignore the vagrant relations among samples, illustrations, and demonstrations in favour of the central feature of a certain class of them all: their *typicality*.

If the task is to show someone how to identify a certain species of weed, one selects representative weed samples—several that are neither "too perfect" nor too marginal—in order to establish the range of properties characteristic of that particular weed. Not every weed in the patch will have all the associated properties depicted in the guidebook to weeds. So unless there are some conspicuous identifying features, it will be necessary to establish the typical range to be found among several instances. "The point of the activity is to pick out all the plants relevantly similar to the example, not merely those most closely resembling the ideal weed". (Silvers, 1978, p. 38) And the point of typical instances is to *be* typical not only of properties invariably possessed but of those sometimes absent. [7]

Models are generally thought to be "unreal" like ship, automobile, or airplane models. We think of them as differing from the real thing in scale, materials, or function. (Howard, 1982, p. 105) Yet we expect them to exemplify certain characteristic features of the real thing. So, for instance, the full-scale clay "mock-up" of a new car may literally exemplify shape, aerodynamics, and size while having none of the mechanical functions of an actual car. Or, as in the case of small-scale "working models", some of the mechanical functions may be exemplified but not size or weight. By contrast, a sample or an exemplar of a car is a real car.

Perhaps then we might say that a model car is not *literally* a car even if it possesses some of the properties of real cars to an exemplary degree. More precisely, a model car is a "car" only metaphorically and therefore metaphorically exemplifies the property of being a car in the same way that a carved decoy, however true-to-life in appearance, cannot literally exemplify the property "being a live duck".

Such an account of the referential functions of models may well apply to many and helps to explain—at least to suggest—their kinship to metaphors[8] and the conceptual grounds of their "unreality" (not literally a car, duck) despite their real usefulness in displaying real aspects of the real thing. But the foregoing account is much too narrow, since not every model is a metaphorical sample. The account also overlooks a more fundamental difference between models and samples while obscuring the peculiar instructional power of models.

Consider the fact that an architect's model used to show the layout, proportions, and materials of a building is neither a metaphor nor a sample of those features. Nor is the surgeon's break-away model of the heart or brain a metaphor or a sample. Rather, such models differ from both samples and descriptions in being nonverbal *labels* denoting the real thing. They belong in the category of nonverbal "telling" quite as much as "showing"—symbols that denote as well as exemplify without describing. (Howard, 1982, pp. 105-106) "Unlike samples", says Goodman, "models are denotative; unlike descriptions, they are nonverbal. Models of this sort are in effect diagrams, often in more than two dimensions and with working parts; or in other words, diagrams are flat and static models." (Goodman, 1972, pp. 172-173) And therein lies the peculiar power of models and diagrams to instruct, namely, in drawing "showing" and "telling" together in one complex symbol having multiple referential functions.[9]

Simulations are usually signalled by such declarations as, "How realistic!" or "That was exactly like the real thing" or "It was as if I were actually there". Simulations, like facsimiles, say, of a medieval manuscript, approximate to the real thing by copying or imitating certain of its features. Nevertheless, like models, simulations however realistic are yet unreal—are not the real thing they are simulating. Which is to say, unlike genuine samples, illustrations, or demonstrations, simulations save appearances at the expense of reality. [10]

Simulations substitute for reality. To the untrained eye, for example, iron pyrite gives the appearance of gold without being gold. A flight trainer duplicates the experience of flight without leaving the ground. A decoy duck looks in water like a real duck, just as an actor on stage may gesture and speak like a real king. All of which suggests a connection between simulation and *pretending* (with or without deception). For being unreal, simulations can be highly realistic in the ways they refer to real worlds, possible worlds, or totally fictional worlds—from mock-ups of moonscapes and museum simulacra, to full scale war games and role playing in group therapy, to the wonderful worlds of Disney and Star Wars.

As well, simulations can symbolise in virtually any way at all: facsimiles of the Magna Carta, of the Portland vase, of the Mona Lisa; brilliants exemplifying the glitter of diamonds; staged debates exemplifying the principles of parliamentary government; film depictions of King Kong scaling the Empire State Building; maps of the Land of Lilliput; diagrams of Captain Nemo's submarine. One may pretend in any symbolic way that one pleases.

Unlike the pretendings of pure fancy, however, simulations retain what might be described as a "pretension" to reality, a certain verisimilitude in experience. From fact to fiction, simulations have a remarkable capacity to foster inquiry, to make discoveries, and to explore possibilities. The point is this: by pretending to be real, simulations expand the powers of imagination and of supposition. Otherwise put, simulations are created to give an *as if* "experience" or "appearance" of the real or imagined thing in ways that circumvent not only the risks but the limitations of everyday reality.

Exemplars, on the other hand, bring us to earth with all the exhilarating force of reality realised at its best. Among examples, exemplars are those which most conspicuously wear their merit on their sleeves. If the task is to show someone how to make a bed, one does it as best one can in order to provide the learner with "an exemplar, an ideal toward which to strive". (Silvers, 1978, p. 38) In other words, exemplars represent the highest normative range of samples, the ideal instances beyond the typical ones.

Not for that reason, however, should ordinary samples and illustrations be considered inferior *examples*; for there are many situations where, as we have seen, insistence on attention to exemplars ("Perfect weeds only, please") would defeat the instructional purpose. What makes examples of any kind "good" or "bad" is how well they serve their cognitive purposes. In that regard, samples and exemplars have different pedagogical roles to play. (Howard, 1972, p. 104)

Nor is exemplar status a matter of how many properties of an example are exemplified, as Silvers seems to suggest. (Silvers, 1978, pp. 38-39) Rather, as I argued elsewhere, "Exemplars closely conform (and perhaps more completely, hence, the suggestion of 'more' properties) to an ideal of some sort. But to exemplify all the requisites of the *ideal* is not the same as exemplifying all the properties of the example. In short, status as an exemplar is not a question of how many, still less of all, properties of an example being exemplified, but of those selected, how *well* they are exemplified". (Howard, 1982, pp. 103-104)

As examples that set an ideal or standard for the learner, exemplars can be divided into two basic types. First are those that establish an ideal in the sense of *fixing* it, like the Standard Yard, the orchestral "A" tuning pitch, or the printmaker's *bon à tirer* which sets the standard for the other prints in an edition. Second are those exemplars that establish an ideal by *furthering* it, like a new scientific discovery, a definitive musical performance, or a better mouse trap. The latter I shall call "open" exemplars and the former "closed" exemplars. [11]

An open exemplar is "open-ended" in the sense that it admits of indefinite further development even as it establishes a high, often new, standard. Janet Baker's performance of Mahler's "Rückert" songs is no less exemplary for failing to be perfect or interpretively different from Jessye Norman's. Besides being unique, both versions are suggestive of new directions of expressive nuance, pointing the way to performance achievements yet unrealised.

Generally speaking, particular facilities, like typing, running scales, or lifting weights, are learned by reference to closed exemplars, where the difference between "right" and "wrong" ways of doing things are relatively straightforward. Whereas, advanced skills involving judgement and choice take the "greyer" measure of progress by reference to open exemplars. Critical assessment, not only of one's approximation to the standard thus set, but of the standard itself never ceases where an open exemplar is in force.

Accordingly, it is an unfortunate mistake when the learner confuses open for closed exemplars, as when the novice soprano says, "I want to sing *exactly* like Janet Baker". What it means to "match" Baker's achievement—to learn from her excellent example—is less a matter in the long run[12] of replicating (in effect, simulating by mimicking) her voice and performance than of doing what Jessye Norman did; namely, find one's own way, perhaps by comparison to what both singers have accomplished.

As with any example, an exemplar may be rivetting or revealing, limiting or liberating, depending upon the quality of instruction, the learner's interpretive ability and level of facilities. We have seen that a certain blindness may set in about one's proficiency or what it means to persist in the pursuit of an ideal—in effect, an estrangement of ends and means. (See Chapter 6) Flailing at an imagined ideal without sufficient preparation or attention to detail is a formula for ruin played out at the extreme of a dream without means. Keeping means and ends connected up then becomes a question of how well we learn to learn from the wider range of examples available to us from sources other than formal instruction.

Reaching Out: Imitation

Kingsley Amis' description in the epigraph to this chapter of how, by a combination of spontaneous attraction, immersion in a literary genre, and blatant imitation, one discovers oneself as a writer has analogues in virtually any field, discipline, or art form. (Amis, 1987, p. vi) It is a matter not only of identifying what is involved in the task, but of identifying *with* it—of taking the pros and cons of the task within oneself in the form of a kind of "inner dialogue".

With something as difficult as writing fiction, the inner dialogue begins with the struggle over whether and how to have a try at it. The products of that dialogue, of course, are public and publicly estimable. But it all starts from a wish to find a way, and the way usually comes from imitating the ways of others. From first imitating the voices of others to finding a voice of one's own is an odyssey by no means peculiar to writers and singers. Swelling that progress is near worshipful imitation, a sometimes maligned form of learning which I am inclined, with qualifications, to celebrate or at least to clarify.

What is imitation? Aside from being the sincerest flattery, imitation is also described in the OED as "following model or example (of); counterfeit". Therein lies the guilt by association from the verb to the noun, from imitating to producing or becoming counterfeit, a "cheap imitation", as we say. Therein too lies the connection to exemplars and other examples from which, if we take Amis' remarks seriously, it does *not* follow that fakes, forgeries, and counterfeits are the inevitable outcomes of imitation—particularly where open exemplars (and capacities) are concerned. Nor would we say that someone who learns to make up a bed by following the example of another is a counterfeit bed-maker or a forger of "hospital corners". There appears to be considerable ground for manoeuvre before imitating *reduces* to cheap imitation.

Imitation is sometimes explained as a species of resemblance. One thing imitates another if the one is closely similar to, copies, highly resembles, or is the same as, the other. But since any two things in the universe are similar in *some* respect, appeals to resemblance to explain imitation are either vacuous or circular. (See Goodman, 1972b, pp. 437-455) Imitation may be piecemeal or wholesale, masterly or slavish, but without specifying in what *respects* the imitation occurs, it is anybody's guess how one thing, person, or action imitates another. That becomes even more apparent where the *attempt* to imitate, say, the precise movements of a dance instructor, fall far short of perfection. Novices at anything difficult are notorious for picking up on the wrong thing.

The idea of imitation as following an example or model suggests another explanation. Construed as an action, as something one does, to imitate is to act with reference to an exemplar, sample, or model with the intent of duplicating the latter within specified limits. (Howard, 1972, p. 109) More than that, an imitative action is one that exemplifies another not only in certain respects but in certain *degrees of approximation* to those respects. That (however vaguely specified) degree of approximation just *is* the degree of resemblance required for the action to be a duplicate—and that can vary wildly with the case.[13] Thus may we account for the facts (a) that imitation occurs in certain degrees as well as in certain respects; and (b) that though built-in, these are highly variable features of imitation. So, it is never enough to say, A imitates B. The queries, How so?, In what ways?, To what degree or extent?, are always appropriate.

I spoke of imitation as involving the "intent", meaning the deliberate attempt, to duplicate something. But of course there are many cases of "unconscious" or involuntary imitation, say, of speech habits or mannerisms picked up by association. (The phenomenon is common enough in the vicinity of charismatic figures, not to mention in every household.) Though unintentional, such cases of imitation are no less referential to the norms by which they are detected. By extension, we also speak of cut glass as imitating diamond, of silk flower imitations, or ersatz coffee. Here too we have in mind specific properties of appearance, of texture, shape, and colour, or of taste that are exemplified by the imitations. And not only do imitations exemplify such properties, but they do so with varying degrees of success: some coffee substitutes are better than others.

The latter point elicits an important feature of imitation as a learning strategy: the *striving* for perfection, as it were; the effort that goes into trying to "live up" to our exemplars and the measures we take of our successes or failures. Such measures, to whatever extent "given" in the exemplars, are taken in (absorbed) by ourselves with varying degrees of accuracy, sensitivity, vision, and diligence. We stand or fall as learners by the ways we aspire to the things we imitate and admire.

That may seem an exaggerated, even melodramatic, pronouncement, but most imitative learning is suspended between two perilous extremes: premature satisfaction and perfectionism. Premature satisfaction amounts to early cut off of the critical faculties through carelessness, an inability to perceive one's mistakes and stage of development, or through falling into the thrall of minor accomplishments.

As Passmore remarks, "Conscientiousness and carefulness may not be the most fascinating of virtues, but virtues they are". (Passmore, 1980, p. 187) Such conscientiousness, he maintains, is to be distinguished from both soppy sentimentality and imagination-destroying pedantry. Far from thwarting imagination, caring for (as well as within) what one is doing is what converts an empty dream into a directed apprenticeship. (Cf. Passmore, 1980, pp. 189-193)

The inability to perceive one's mistakes and stage of development is endemic to many advanced skills, as we have seen. Hence the necessity of another eye or ear—of an instructor or coach—to monitor one's progress, detect hidden errors, and suggest corrections. Hence too the dangers of complacency, in this case, the obverse of blindness to error in the form of thralldom to a minor success. A ringing high "C" at the expense of everything else does not an aria make any more than a single swallow makes a spring—a lesson, incidentally, that Mario Lanza, the popular tenor of the fifties, never did learn.

Opposite to premature satisfaction lie the shoals of perfectionism, an excess of caring to the extent of neurotic anxiety. The perfectionist puts himself in the unenviable position of having to get everything right to the highest degree straightaway. A common enough source of so-called "writer's block" (See Howard and Barton, 1986, pp. 22-25), perfectionism has been demonstrated to diminish learning efficiency as well as the quality and quantity of output. (Burns, 1985, pp. 300-323) Loathing error in any form, perfectionism eliminates the lessons to be learned from mistakes while extinguishing the capacity for risk-taking.

Yet a fertile area remains between the extremes of premature satisfaction and perfectionism where imitation does its best work by enabling us to exceed precedent even as we strive to adhere to it. Mr. Barth, the baritone from an earlier chapter, sought to imitate the "smelling of a flower" as he executed a difficult vocal passage. In so doing, his exertions exemplified a metaphor in the service of yet another metaphor: the "open throat".[14] The literal inspanning of his pharanx followed as a matter of course, giving him a purchase on what to do. Had Mr. Barth lacked the imagination to grasp the metaphor *in mime-action*, he would have failed conspicuously. His failure of imitation would have been as evident as his vocal failure. Yet, the moment he grasped the point of the metaphor, he was liberated to be himself vocally in a way that goes beyond slavish adherence to precept or example in much the same way (thought no doubt more slowly and on a grander scale) that Amis' "imitation" led to a literary voice of his own.

How does one get beyond imitation? The quick answer is, by imitation itself, by practising what one aspires to. We have already seen that proper practise transforms means and ends-in-view. That is, the very idea of what we aspire to alters with growing competence. Otherwise, we should be locked into a drudgery of ends as well as of means. That can and does often happen, and the result is indeed "cheap imitation", as witness the horde of Elvis Presley clones in the pop music world. But if the escape from imitation is through imitation, by what *further* process do we get beyond established precedent? Again, the quick answer is, by reexamining the examples—especially the exemplars—before us and adjusting them to our own circumstances—by, as it were, taking them in rather than being taken in by them. I shall call this process extrapolation.

Reaching Beyond: Extrapolation

The ordinary meaning of extrapolation is to calculate approximately from known values or data to others lying beyond the range of those known. That is the meaning adopted herein but generalised so as to include, without being limited to, tricks and formulae. So, for instance, on the proposed usage extrapolation refers not only to the ability to continue a number series (3, 6, 9, 12 . . . n) but to the abilities to take a hint, to learn from examples, and, most importantly, to escape the bonds of received knowledge and precedent. It is the latter variety that most concerns us here.

First, another anecdote. Nicolai Gedda, one of my two favourite operatic tenors (the other being the late Jussi Bjoerling) was interviewed by baritone Jerome Hines in a book entitled *Great Singers on Great Singing* (1982, pp. 188-125). Commenting on his vocal training and technique, Gedda said, "My first teacher [Oehman] taught that the position of the throat, when singing, should be the same position you have when you are yawning: wide open and without any muscles . . . no tension whatsoever. So I think you should forget about the throat. By inhaling properly, as when you yawn, your Adam's apple automatically goes into a low position . . . Now, I don't just take a breath and exercise. I do a whole procedure. I have the mouth closed and I inhale . . . not through the nostrils only . . . but deeper, so I have a sensation behind the nose." "'I hear a slight sighing sound', I [Hines] said. 'You try to produce a sinus resonance as you inhale?' 'Exactly', was his [Gedda's] enthusiastic reply. 'And that gives me the sensation that, when I start to sing, I already have the mask open'". A little later in the interview, Gedda repeated the point about inhaling. "'And every exercise I do this . . . ' He demonstrated again the slow breathing through the nose. 'She [his second teacher, Novicova] also taught me the *sorriso* [smile] position of the mouth . . . a *slight* smile'". (Hines, 1982, pp. 120-121 and 123)

Not long after reading this interview, I had occasion to see Gedda at close range performing Berlioz's *Faust* in concert with the Boston Symphony Orchestra. Seated with the other soloists, as the moment approached for him to sing his first lines, he seemed almost withdrawn with a Buddha-like expression on his face. I also noticed a slight twitching of his cheeks which increased as he stood up, very straight, his lips curling upwards at the corners. Then, of course, it struck me: he's *inhaling*, and there—the Buddha grimace—is the *sorriso*! It was one of the best "voice lessons" of my life.

I say "voice lesson" because this was an example more taken than given and a "lesson" only in the sense that I made it so. Equipped with the above interview in the back of my mind and with a special interest in vocal technique, Gedda's performance was for me on that occasion as much a demonstration as a musical performance. Back in the practice studio, I grimaced and twitched and inhaled much as he had done and found to my surprise that it worked: I was able to achieve a better "placed" tone than my normal one, nothing like Gedda's unfortunately, but better.

Now except for the details specific to singing, this is not an uncommon experience. It is, in fact, typical of the ways we learn from examples and exemplars supplied by the professional, scientific, or artistic worlds we inhabit—provided we are in a position to interpret and incorporate what we find there. Merely to have imitated Gedda's twitches and grimaces would not have been enough. As auto-suggestive mannerisms, it's what lay *behind* them in the way of technical know-how that counted. His earlier words and living example awakened a physical insight later facilitated by imitating his actual mannerisms. Without that insight, without the *context* of his description and my own vocal experience, imitating him would have been little more than caricature. Mistaking symptom for substance is one of the more common ways that imitation can misfire.

One of the aims of instruction in any field is to enable the learner to distinguish symptom from substance: to see the difference between the romantic social image and the reality that lies behind it. With proper guidance, imitation is one of the more powerful means at our disposal for negotiating that passage. Without proper guidance, imitation, like unfettered fancy, is rootless and banal—one might say, "route-less", lacking a sense of direction. And it is that dawning sense of direction provided by open exemplars that points the learner beyond the done thing.

Earlier, I spoke of imitation as always being in certain respects and in certain degrees of approximation to those respects. In effect, *deliberate* imitation is both selective and interpretive, requiring an exercise of judgement and choice about what and how much to imitate. Even "slavish" imitation, say, of the pronunciation of foreign words in language learning, requires one to monitor a number of variables at once: inflection, vowel and consonant sounds, rhythm, and so forth. Like drill, imitation can be bovine or bounteous depending upon the intelligence with which it is done. Moreover, as a frequent component of drill and practise generally, imitation may acquire the perspective of the larger tasks and disciplines they serve. In other words, there is nothing *inherently* opposed to the spirit of inquiry in the activity of imitation. Viewed in such perspective, routines and procedures learned by imitation invite extrapolation to the unknown. And like the other patterns of exemplification discussed in this chapter, imitation has as much to show us as our backgrounds and experience enables us to see.

Having briefly reconnoitred in the preceding chapters the terrains of imagination, expression, and learning by instruction, practice, and example, in the final chapter I want to return to the rather elusive topic with which I began: the "aesthetics" of learning, somewhat along Shillerian lines, but in more prosaic terms under the heading of Learning by Reflection.

Notes

1 On the relations among labels, properties, and possession, see Goodman, 1972, pp. 54-67.

2 On the emphemerality of symbol functions in some circumstances, see Goodman, 1978, pp. 66-67.

3 For Goodman, a predicate or description is a label in a linguistic system. Labels may also be nonlinguistic and both kinds may be exemplified. (See Goodman, 1972, p. 57)

4 I am using 'verbal' here to mean *linguistic*, spoken or written. Earlier on, I used it to contrast *oral* from written language. See p. 3 above.

5 Recall Black's remark that "The nearer we come to what is readily *seen* by an apt learner, the harder it becomes to articulate the governing rule and a point is soon reached at which the effort of attending to the verbal formula positively interferes with the primary performance." See Chapter 5, pp. 80-81 above. "Lower" is not a difficult verbal formula to fathom, but what it entails in a properly executed knee-bend may be better seen in action than described.

6 I am endebted here to Anita Silvers' (1978) exemplificational analysis of samples, models, and exemplars. See also Howard (1982), pp. 102-112.

7 Which is why, incidentally, field guides to birds and wild flowers make special note of young as well as mature plumages, spring blossoms as well as leaf shapes. Depending upon the time of year, you take your choice of identifying features.

8 Including the kinships to simile (or literal likeness), to understatement (e.g. simplified ship models), and to overstatement (e.g., the dentist's outsize model of a tooth). Cf. Goodman, (1972), pp. 77-78; and pp. 81-85. On the general topic of models and metaphors, including scientific and logico-mathematical models not discussed here, see Black (1962) and Turbayne (1962).

9 Israel Scheffler speaks of certain "quasi-denotative uses" of a term as "mention-selective . . . in a manner reminscent of metaphor". For example, when we apply the term 'man' to select not a man but a man-picture (a man in the picture), "we here apply the term not to what it denotes

but rather to a mention thereof". (Scheffler, 1979, pp. 34-35) Similarly, when saying of a tooth model, "This is a tooth", one refers to it *as* as tooth—a case of mention-selection. One is not only singling out the model but giving the learner the basis of generalising to other models the teacher might use. In effect, the learner acquires a whole system of denoting objects from which to learn more about the world of teeth. See also Howard (1980).

10 As mentioned, models and simulations sometimes overlap, sometimes not. Roughly, a full scale mock-up of a car simulating the form, colour, and size of the car is also a model. A toy car is a model but not a simulator; and a fake jewel is a simulator (facsimile) but not a model.

11 By analogy to Passmore's "open" and "closed" capacities. See Chapter 6, footnote 8 above. The difference in this connection between a capacity and an exemplar (or any example, for that matter) is that a capacity, like volleying in tennis, need not symbolise anything and may be done well or badly; whereas an exemplar of volleying is an instance of volleying used to exemplify the best in volleying.

12 Even though in the short run imitation of another's achievements *may* enhance the growth of particular facilities. See the remarks of Kingsley Amis in the epigraph to this Chapter as well as the following section.

13 On the difference between duplicates and replicas in symbol theory, see Goodman (1972), p. 131n.

14 It is worth noting in passing that imitation may be of things literal or metaphoric, simple or complex, large or small scale.

References

Kingsley Amis, *The Crime of the Century* (London: J. M. Dent, 1987).

Max Black, *Models and Metaphors* (Ithaca: Cornell University Press, 1962).

Max Black, "Rules and Routines", in R. S. Peters (ed.), *The Concept of Education* (London: Routledge and Kegan Paul, 1967).

Benjamin S. Bloom, "Automaticity, the Hands and Feet of Genius", *Educational Leadership*, February 1986, pp. 70-77.

David D. Burns, *Feeling Good, The New Mood Therapy* (New York: William Morrow, 1980).

Nelson Goodman, *Languages of Art, An Approach to a Theory of Symbols* (Indianapolis: Hackett, 1972).

Nelson Goodman, "Seven Strictures on Similarity", in *Problems and Projects* (Indianapolis: Hackett, 1972b).

Nelson Goodman, *Ways of Worldmaking* (Indianapolis: Hackett, 1978).

Howard E. Gruber, "Creativity and the Constructive Function of Repetition", English manuscript in typescript published in French as, "Creativité et fonction constructif de la répétition", *Bulletin de Psychologie de la Sorbonne*, 1976.

Jerome Hines, *Great Singers on Great Singing* (New York: Doubleday, 1982).

V. A. Howard, Review of Israel Scheffler, *Beyond the Letter, A Philosophical Inquiry into Ambiguity, Vagueness, and Metaphor in Language,* in *Harvard Educational Review,* vol. 51, no 3, August 1981.

V. A. Howard, *Artistry, the Work of Artists* (Indianapolis: Hackett, 1982).

V. A. Howard and J. H. Barton, *Thinking on Paper* (New York: William Morrow, 1986).

John Passmore, *The Philosophy of Teaching* (Cambridge: Harvard University Press, 1980).

Gilbert Ryle, *The Concept of Mind* (Chicago: University of Chicago Press, 1984); first published in 1949.

Israel Scheffler, *Beyond the Letter, A Philosophical Inquiry into Ambiguity, Vagueness, and Metaphor in Language* (London: Routledge & Kegan Paul, 1979).

Anita Silvers, "Show and Tell: The Arts, Cognition, and Basic Modes of Referring", in S. S. Madeja (ed.), *The Arts, Cognition, and Basic Skills* (St. Louis: CEMREL, 1978).

C. M. Turbayne, *The Myth of Metaphor* (New Haven: Yale University Press, 1962).

8

Learning by Reflection

Where there is reflection there is suspense.
—John Dewey

The Aesthetics of Learning

In *Art as Experience*, John Dewey describes a perfectly ordinary experience in quite extraordinary terms.

"Two men meet: one is the applicant for a position, while the other has the disposition of the matter in his hands. The interview may be mechanical, consisting of set questions, the replies to which perfunctorily settle the matter. There is no experience in which the two men meet, nothing that is not a repetition, by way of acceptance or dismissal, of something which has happened a score of times. The situation is disposed of as if it were an exercise in bookkeeping. But an interplay may take place in which a new experience develops. Where should we look for an account of such an experience? Not to ledger-entries nor yet to a treatise on economics or sociology or personnel-psychology, but to drama or fiction.[1] Its nature and import can be expressed only by art, because there is a unity of experience that can be expressed only as an experience.[2] The *experience* is of material fraught with suspense and moving toward its own consummation through a connected series of varied incidents. The primary emotions on the part of the applicant may be at the beginning hope or despair, and elation or disappointment at the close. These emotions qualify the experience as a unity. But as the interview proceeds, secondary emotions are evolved as variations of the primary underlying one. It is even possible for each attitude and gesture, each sentence, almost every word, to produce more than a fluctuation in the intensity of the basic emotion; to produce, that is, a change of shade and tint in its quality. The employer sees by means of his own emotional reactions the character of the one applying. He projects him imaginatively into the work to be done and judges his fitness by the way in which the elements of the scene assemble and either clash or fit together. The presence and behaviour of the applicant either harmonize with his own attitudes and desires or they conflict and jar. Such factors as these, inherently esthetic in quality, are the forces that carry the varied elements of the interview to a decisive issue. They

enter into the settlement of every situation, whatever its dominant
nature, in which there are uncertainty and suspense."
(Dewey, 1934, pp. 42-43)

A job interview as an aesthetic experience? That seems rather
farfetched, to say the least. Art and utility are traditional oppo-
sites, if not enemies, are they not? Mr. Common Sense knows
better than to confuse effete art with practical matters. He
never lets his passing interest in art as "an affair for odd
moments" (Dewey, 1934, p. 54) intrude upon his urgency to fill
the unforgiving moment of business.

As usual where theory comes into play, Mr. Common Sense
lacks the subtlety to see the secrets of his own success. He does
with gusto what he does not understand, and more power to
him; but we must not let ourselves be deceived by his "bottom
line", ends-focussed, thinking. He plays a role in the drama
with perceptive sensitivity, and yet does not understand the
play. He wants results; we want an explanation of how he gets
them. He seeks convenient means; we seek general understanding of how they work. These are quite different motives, quite
different outlooks; and Dewey is onto those differences in a way
that unites practical, intellectual, and aesthetic perceptions of a
situation.

An experience, such as the job interview related above, as
something which departs from the humdrum of the neutrally
passing scene, "has a unity that gives it its name, *that* meal, that
storm, that rupture of friendship." (1934, p. 37) And then, in a
passage strongly reminiscent of Schiller's *spieltrieb* in mature
judgement (See Chapter 1, p. 5 above), Dewey says, "This . . .
unity is constituted by a single *quality* that pervades the entire
experience in spite of the variation of its constituent parts. This
unity is neither emotional, practical, nor intellectual, for these
terms name distinctions that reflection can make within it."
(1934, p. 37)

This is more than an argument in praise of the specifically
"cognitive emotions" like the joy of fulfilled expectation or
surprise (See Scheffler, 1986), and less than a call for an
"education of the emotions" as such. (See Peters, 1972) For,
Dewey is suggesting that all thinking and thoughtful action, as
experienced moment to moment, are emotionally qualified.

"There are absorbing inquiries and speculations which a scientific man and philosopher will recall as 'experiences' in the emphatic sense. In final import they are intellectual. But in their actual occurrence they were emotional as well; they were purposive and volitional". (1934, p. 37) Even the drawing of a logical conclusion from premises—as a lived experience—is "a movement of anticipation and culmination, one that finally comes to completion. A 'conclusion' is no separate and independent thing; it is the consummation of a movement". (1934, p. 38) Consequently, "*an* experience of thinking", Dewey maintains, "has its own esthetic quality. It differs from those experiences that are acknowledged to be esthetic, but only in its materials". (1934, p. 38) And yet more emphatically, " . . . the esthetic is no intruder in experience from without, whether by way of idle luxury or transcendent reality . . . it is the clarified and intensified development of traits that belong to every normally complete experience". (1934, p. 46) "In short, esthetic cannot be sharply marked off from intellectual experience since the latter must bear an esthetic stamp to be itself complete". (1934, p. 38)

If I understand him correctly, Dewey is saying that the "aesthetic stamp" may exist in different degrees of imprint, no doubt most conspicuously in art but elsewhere too: in practical and intellectual experience; not merely as a patina upon those experiences but as a seamless ingredient of them, what in these pages I call getting the proper "feel" of a skill, discipline, or situation, or Wittgenstein's "nose" for something.

For example, in a passage that could well have been written by Schiller, Dewey comments on the aesthetic quality of moral action. "One great defect in what passes as morality is its anesthetic quality. Instead of exemplifying wholehearted action, it takes the form of grudging piecemeal concessions to the demands of duty". (1934, p. 39) Even nowadays, perhaps especially in these days of anaesthetic "basics" and other so-called "cognitive skills", Dewey's remarks on the aesthetic face of thinking, of morals, and of experience generally are tantamount to pedagogical heresy, if not revolution.

Dewey shares that distinction with Herbert Read, who goes even further in elaborating "the aesthetic basis of discipline and morality" in his *Education Through Art* (1945). Towards the end of that eloquent book, Read places himself squarely in the footsteps of Plato and Schiller.

> Plato meant exactly what he said: that an aesthetic education is the only education that brings grace to the body and nobility to the mind, and that we must make art the basis of education because it can operate in childhood, during the sleep of reason; and when reason does come, art will have prepared a path for her, and she will be greeted as a friend whose essential lineaments have for long been familiar. Moreoever, Plato did not see or offer any alternative to art as an instrument of early education—it is the only instrument that can penetrate into the recesses of the soul. Plato's teaching on this matter was taken up in the modern world by Schiller, and in all his philosophical works, but above all in his *Letters upon the Aesthetical Education of Man* [sic], we have again a clear and explicit statement of this doctrine of education: that until man, in his physical and sensuous modes of being, has been accustomed to the laws of beauty, he is not capable of perceiving what is good and true—he is not capable of spiritual liberty. Many other witnesses to this truth might be called but none so unequivocal as these two, whom I value more than any others; and I am very content to rest in their company. (Read, 1945, pp. 277-278)

Independent of Dewey's and Read's views, the narrower issue of the aesthetic in otherwise *non-artistic* experience is two-fold: first, what is "aesthetic"—and in what sense of the word—about reflective thought and action generally; and second, how does that enter into learning by all the means previously discussed? The following sections focus upon these two questions.

I hesitate to use the phrase, "the aesthetics of learning", but I'm afraid I shall to refer to a side of learning that is as much a matter of sensibility and taste as of reason and judgement. The only solace I can offer in broaching such an odd slant on learning is that most of what I have to say about it has already been said in one way or other in previous chapters; so this is my last opportunity to draw those threads together in a rough historical weave.

Why I am not a Kantian on Sensibility

The key terms in pursuit of the two questions before us are "the aesthetic" and "sensibility", the one referring to a predominantly symbolic feature of things and events, the other referring to an interpretive activity of mind mediated by symbols. First, sensibility.

My use of the term 'sensibility' stands in marked contrast to the Kantian use and its implications for aesthetic experience. For Kant, any judgement leading to knowledge involves the operation of two irreducible mental faculties: understanding and sensibility. The former is an active faculty of "concepts"; whereas the latter is a passive faculty of "intuitions" (*Anschauugen*), the sum of all impingements upon a normal sensory apparatus—everything we get through the five senses. Though different, understanding and sensibility "can supply objectively valid judgements of things only in *conjunction* with each other". (Kant, 1781, A p. 271, B p. 327) Without concepts we could not think; without sensory data we should have nothing to think about. (Cf. Scruton, 1982, p. 25)

Suppose, for example, I say, "There is a clock on the wall". For that judgement to be "objective"—literally, to refer to an object in experience—I must subsume the sensory data of my eyes under the concepts of "clock" and "wall". "Without sensibility no object would be given to us, without understanding no object would be thought. Thoughts without content are empty; intuitions without concepts are blind." (Kant, 1781, A p. 51, B p. 75) Experience, then, is a "synthesis" of concepts and intuitions (1781, A p. 79, B p. 104), a mental sandwich, as it were, put together out of an active faculty that construes via concepts and a passive faculty that merely collects "data" *via* the five senses.

Carrying this view of thoughtless sensibility as ingredient to perceptual experience into the domain of the aesthetic, what are we to make of my experience, say, of the beauty of a tulip? (Kant's own example) According to Kant, such an experience is of the immediate pleasure felt, unmediated by concepts, in perceiving the tulip. (Kant, 1790, p. 141) Such an experience has "merely subjective validity" and the judgement that the tulip is beautiful is merely "one of taste, and not one of understanding or reason". (Kant, 1790, pp. 140-141) Yet precisely because we judge the tulip to *be* beautiful, we seem to lay claim to universal assent. This impasse engenders the famous "antinomy of taste".

"1. *Thesis.* The judgement of taste is not based upon concepts; for if it were, it would be open to dispute (decision by means of proofs).

2. *Antithesis.* The judgement of taste is based on concepts; for otherwise, despite diversity of judgement, there could be no room even for contention in the matter (a claim to the necessary agreement of others with this judgement)." (Kant, 1790, p. 206)

This is hardly the place to launch a discussion of Kant's solution to the antinomy of taste in terms of synthetic *a priori* judgements (ones that are prior to experience yet factual). (1790, p. 145ff) The gist of that solution is that concepts like "Beauty" come into play only in thinking *about* aesthetic experiences not *in* them. However, I am less concerned to pursue details thoroughly examined by others than to contrast Kant's view of sensibility, one still powerfully influential, with my own. Suffice to say that in Kant's own final analysis, there are no valid principles of taste (1790, p. 141); we are left with a presumptive "as if" perception of Beauty in the tulip in virtue of which we are merely "suitors for agreement from everyone else". (1790, p. 82) The pleasures of aesthetic experience being immediate, bypassing reason, concepts, and analysis, sensibility is thereby stripped of all cognitive function. As Roger Scruton puts it, "It seems that it is always [sensory] experience, and never conceptual thought, that gives the right to aesthetic judgement . . . " (Scruton, 1982, p. 81)

Now it is one thing to say that art, or aesthetic perception, is especially a matter of sensory experience. That may well be. It is quite another to assert that such experience is necessarily "free from concepts"; that sensibility is only a receptor faculty "taking in" whatever it is given. Besides begging the question of the "given" in perception (Cf. Goodman, 1972, pp. 8-9), Kant reduces sensibility—by my account, an interpretive activity—to immutable sensory stimulation or *mere* sensation.

Kant's original dichotomy of understanding and sensibility of course underlies the antinomy of taste. And underlying the dichotomy is the assumption of immutable sensibility. Without accepting the dichotomy, one can yet sympathise with its motive; namely, that something independent of concepts is required to control our conceptualisations, to *ground* them. That is, we create concepts by which to catch experience, and in so doing, put constraints upon that experience which in turn constrains our fancy. There is no preestablished harmony between thought and reality. The world is not just anything we think it to be. Yet in casting our conceptual nets upon the world we need not assume that only immutable sensory fish will come up in them: that whatever is "given" in sensory experience is unalterable by conceptualisation.

A wealth of psychological experiment points to the opposite view.[3] Bruner for one in a well known study has shown that the perceived size of coins may vary with estimates of their value. (Bruner, 1947, 43-56) Then there is the common experience of "normalising" the image projected on a cinema screen when viewed at an acute angle. Such phenomena support a more *interactive* relation between understanding and sensibility than Kant allows. As Scheffler remarks, "We simply have a false dichotomy in the notion that observation must be either a pure confrontation with an undifferentiated given, or else so conceptually contaminated that it must render circular any observational test of a hypothesis." (Scheffler, 1982, p. 39) If, then, sensibility is construed as an active, interpretive *form* of understanding, very much alive with "concepts" (I prefer to say symbolically mediated), both Kant's antinomy of taste and the original dichotomy of understanding and sensibility disappear.

However cavalier these remarks on Kant's aesthetic, they are nonetheless *arguable* points suggesting a quite different view of sensibility within and without the arts. Two of the dictionary meanings of 'sensibility' are "the capacity to feel" (physical sensations), and "exceptional openness to emotional impressions". (OED) To the latter, emotional impressions, I would add many others of the sort required, for instance, to "read the signals" in Dewey's business interview above. Accordingly, to say of someone that he or she has lost all sensibility could mean either that a capacity to feel physical stimuli has been lost, or that a certain sensitivity about what is going on in a given situation is absent or blunted. To impugn one's ability to listen does not imply a hearing loss any more than the inability to see the face in a picture puzzle implies a sight deficit. The former, discriminatory capacities, are interpretive forms of sensibility, involving concepts, symbols, and subtle uses of judgement and understanding.

As an ingredient of aesthetic or other experience, sensibility is filtered through a variety of symbolic systems engendering a wide array of "concepts" stretching far beyond descriptive or depictive world versions to include the many forms of expression and exemplification aforementioned. That in turn implies that sensibility is not a segregated faculty standing on its own awaiting "synthesis" by yet another faculty of understanding. Rather, sensibility is a form of understanding, itself a "synthesizer" of signs, signals, and clues variously cloaked, often inchoate, and requiring reflective effort to interpret.

So, why am I not a Kantian on the question of aesthetic or other kinds of sensibility? Because it seems that the Kantian analysis leads to a constricting view of the arts and of aesthetic experience generally, particularly their connections to ordinary life. Thoughtless sensibility suggests the idea of the artist (or aesthetic perceiver) as enthralled by the sensory surface of things, bent on simple pleasure, cut off from all conceptual world versions and awareness, while simultaneously questing after a formalistic kind of Beauty (via synthetic *a priori* judgements) having little to do with the "real" worlds of ordinary experience and science. Moreoever, the notion that aesthetic judgement does not apply to objective nature renders art as much "an affair for odd moments" as ever enjoyed by Gilbert and Sullivan's Bunthorne wafted away "in a high aesthetic line".

Symptoms of Significance

What is "aesthetic" about reflective thought and action? How does sensibility come into play? I disagree with Dewey that the aesthetic comes down to "emotional quality" and the subtlety with which we detect it (1934, p. 38) for the reasons given in Chapter 3. The aesthetic encompasses much more than the experience, perception, or expression of emotions. Surely the feeling tone of the job interview described above is an important ingredient of it, but what goes under the label, "feeling tone", is more than emotion. It includes a host of "readings" of the nuances of the situation all of which are symbolically mediated in a variety of ways: facial expressions, postures ("body language"), tones of voice, gestures, not to mention what actually gets said, or meant if not actually said.

Like a work of art, the job interview is replete with patterns of exemplification and expression that convey the overall (in this instance, non-artistic) message. It takes a degree of connoisseurship in such matters to interpret the full range of symbolic activity involved.

To acknowledge such connoisseurship does not turn a practical matter into a work of art as a novelist might do. Nor does it reduce business acumen to "aesthetic" understanding or perception. Still less does it bend the uses of the symbolic systems involved in the job interview to artistic ends. Quite the contrary. Yet, to acknowledge such connoisseurship is to recognise that many of the same patterns of reference, perception, and understanding as occur in art occur elsewhere, indeed are ubiquitous in everyday life. Even as it is impossible to draw a sharp line between art and non-art within the domain of the aesthetic, so also it is futile to try to sharply demarcate the aesthetic from the non-aesthetic in ordinary affairs. (Cf. Howard, 1982, pp. 14-17) Some "symptoms" of the aesthetic crop up virtually everywhere. This requires some explanation.

Goodman avers five symptoms of the aesthetic; which is to say, logical/referential features of symbols functioning aesthetically. I will give them first in his words and then in mine. He says,

" . . . I venture the tentative thought that there are five symptoms of the aesthetic: (1) syntactic density, where the finest differences in certain respects constitute a difference between symbols—for example an ungraduated thermometer as contrasted with an electronic digital-read-instrument; (2) semantic density, where symbols are provided for things distinguished by the finest differences in certain respects—for example, not only the ungraduated thermometer again but also ordinary English, though it is not syntactically dense; (3) relative repleteness, where comparatively many aspects of a symbol are significant—for example, a single-line drawing of a mountain by Hokusai where every feature of shape, line, thickness, etc. counts, in contrast with perhaps the same line as a chart of daily stockmarket averages, where all that counts is the heights of the line above the base; (4) exemplification, where a symbol, whether or not it denotes, symbolizes by serving as a sample of properties it literally or metaphorically possesses; and finally (5) multiple and complex reference, where a symbol performs several integrated and interacting referential functions, some direct and some mediated through other symbols." (Goodman, 1978, pp. 67-68; see also Goodman 1972, pp. 252-255)

For the benefit of those readers unfamiliar with Goodman's technical vocabulary of symbol theory, I shall attempt to restate the symptoms of the aesthetic in simpler (but of course less precise) terms. Syntactic and semantic density of symbols together refer to the subtlety and nuance of symbols, how *fine grained*, one might say, are the symbols themselves and the meanings they convey. The slightest shading of hue or of tone, for example, can transform a painting or musical performance. Repleteness is easier to grasp, referring to the number of features of the symbol that *count* as carrying meaning: the Hoksusai line *versus* the graph line. Exemplification we have already discussed as a kind of *showing forth*, expressively or otherwise; or, even more loosely put, the usually unannounced ways in which a symbol draws attention to itself. (See Chapter 7, pp. 111-113 above) Finally, multiple reference is just that, the sheer *weight* of meaning conveyed in perhaps several different ways at once: for example, Robert Indiana's sculptured word, 'Love', or an illuminated manuscript that are both visual art as well as words.

Together, these symptoms of the aesthetic tend to emphasise the "nontransparency" of works of art, how they arrest our attention by their details of structure, meaning, and expression in ways that traffic signs, clock faces, or plain language do not. The latter having delivered their messages, we tend to ignore the medium. Or as Goodman puts it, in art "we cannot merely look through the symbol to what it refers to as we do in obeying traffic lights or reading scientific texts, but must attend constantly to the symbol itself as in seeing paintings or reading poetry". (Goodman, 1978, p. 69)

Such "primacy of the work [of the symbol itself] over what it refers to" (p. 69) in art is exactly the opposite of the job interview situation, of course. One would hardly dream of asking the interviewer, "Oh please, sir, would you repeat that question, in just that tone of voice? It was so darkly sinister and pregnant with menace!" And it would be tantamount to insult to remark at the end, "What a splendid performance you gave—each line perfectly inflected, the intimidation so exquisitely restrained yet evident in your every gesture". Yet these *are* the sorts of things we learn to notice in real life situations in ways suggesting that life mirrors art at least as often as the reverse.

I already noted, with Dewey, that the "aesthetic stamp" can exist in different degrees of imprint in ordinary (non-artistic) experience. What literal sense can we make of this claim? One suggestion comes from Goodman's commentary on his "symptoms". "These symptoms", he says, "provide no definition [of art or the aesthetic] . . . Symptoms, after all, are but clues; the patient may have the symptoms without the disease, or the disease without the symptoms. And even for these five symptoms to come somewhere near being disjunctively necessary and conjunctively (as a syndrom) sufficient might well call for some redrawing of the vague and vagrant borderlines of the aesthetic". (Goodman, 1978, pp. 68-69)

To put the matter simply (and all too roughly), the convergence of all these symptoms in an object or event is likely to render such object or event as recognizably "aesthetic". Yet they may occur individually or in various combinations virtually anywhere. If, as we say, "clothes make the man or woman", a large corporation will have a dress code because of what that mode of dress is supposed to exemplify in the way of seriousness, competence, professionalism, and the like. Similarly, the interviewer may express his or her attitude toward the applicant by all the means aforementioned: tone of voice, choice of words, facial expressions, or gestures.

Take tone of voice. The interviewer asks, "And just what experience have you in this area?" uttered with a scornful sneer. The question is hardly a neutral request for information. It is *replete* with suggestion (everything—the words, the sneer, the inflection, the timing, counts), simultaneously *exemplifying* an attitude of scorn, semantically *dense* with meaning far beyond the literal gist of the question.

No work of art, surely, the query nonetheless displays several of the symbol functions of art works. The point being that learning to "read" such a loaded query is on a continuum with learning to read poetry, or Shakespeare. The messages and the objectives may differ drastically, but many of the cognitive and symbolic "mechanisms" are the same. A clever medical diagnostician or interviewer is as astute a reader of patients or personalities as any critic of works of art. That is the "aesthetic stamp" on the interviewer's question above: a sensitivity to meaning in all its varieties and symbolic means of conveyance. Learning to "read the signs" in any field or situation is an education of sensibility and judgement. That may not be art, but it is artful. [4]

On Second Thought: Reflections on Reflection

If the preceding gives some indication of what might be vagrantly "aesthetic" about reflective thought and action, what is reflection anyway? Dewey describes "reflective thought" as "Active, persistent, and careful consideration of any belief or supposed form of knowledge in the light of the grounds that support it and further conclusions to which it tends." (Dewey, 1933, p. 118; italics omitted)

Well enough, perhaps, as a general description except that Dewey also opposes such thinking to "Tradition, instruction, imitation—all of which depend upon authority in some form, or appeal to our own advantage, or fall in with a strong passion . . . Such thoughts are prejudices; that is, prejudgements, not conclusions reached as the result of personal mental activity, such as observing, collecting, and examining evidence". (1933, p. 116)

Ever the opponent of hardening of the categories, Dewey nonetheless erects a number of false dichotomies here. One senses the same zeal that, at the opposite extreme, makes him suspicious of "pure fancy". (See Chapter 6, pp. 96-97 above) Having spent the greater part of this book defending the personal, critical, and imaginative dimensions of tradition, instruction, imitation, and authority, I cannot agree that the latter necessarily, or only, issue in prejudice and prejudgement; nor that they fail to observe and weigh evidence; nor that reflective thought is either alien to or opposed to them. On the contrary, I am inclined to the view that the *achievement* of reflective thought in any given domain is virtually impossible without tradition, instruction, imitation, and some measure of authority. But having already had my say on those topics above and on certain shortcomings in Dewey's analysis of reflective thinking elsewhere (Howard, 1988, pp. 7-12), I prefer to start afresh. [5]

What I am calling learning by reflection has more to do with second than first thoughts. That certainly puts me in the *vicinity* of Dewey who also describes reflective thinking as "the kind of thinking that consists in turning a subject over in the mind and giving it serious and consecutive consideration". (Dewey, 1933, p. 113) But I am not at all in the business of recommending "a better way" of doing it. I shall be satisfied to understand a bit of what is involved in anybody's doing it, well or badly.

One sense of reflection is roughly synonymous with 'rethinking' or 'reconsideration'. We often say, "On reflection, I doubt whether I was right"; or, "On Second thought, perhaps it should be this way"; or, "Reconsidering the matter, I should have acted differently"; or, "Act in haste, repent at leisure", to warn against the consequences of insufficient reflection. We do not always have the luxury of mulling things over (and just as well *sometimes*). Time and chance may not allow "going back in thought", consulting with oneself or another, before a decision must be made, a conclusion drawn, an action undertaken; but most learning situations do allow sufficient latitude for the sharpening of foresight by the scrutiny of insight and hindsight. We call this "reconsideration", "reflective thought", or just "second thoughts" to contrast them with our first thoughts and impulses which might have taken us in quite different directions.

Certainly there is no sharp line to be drawn between first and second thoughts.[6] The distinction is both relative and one of convenience; and here, as elsewhere in these pages, we are dealing as much with an attitude of mind—a disposition—as with particular facilities. To be a reflective person in this sense is to be *prone* to reconsider things carefully.

Still, reconsideration does imply some prior consideration, some first acquaintance with the matter at hand that prompts further reflection, a second, longer or deeper look: such phenomena of the imagination previously discussed as mental rehearsal, reliving an experience in memory, concocting an illustration, imagining changes in a musical composition, painting, or work of fiction. Supposition also comes into play in reconsidering the steps of a logical or mathematical proof, in reviewing a legal decision, in assessing a military or political strategy, in making economic projections, or in educational planning. Certainly practise is, or can be, a reflective activity as is learning by example, particularly the exemplars we choose to emulate. A good deal of second thinking is the replaying and revising of first thoughts (and actions) with added information or with alternatives in view that may have been missed the first time around.

There is yet another sense of reflection, akin to 'reconsideration' or 'rethinking', but closer in analogy to the physical meaning of the word as when we speak of reflected light, colour, heat, sound, or objects. It concerns what I shall call professional or personal "style" and what the world of work and achievement reflects back to us if we but have the eyes and minds to see it. In the words of Theodor Reik, speaking of the same phenomenon in another context, "The psychoanalyst has to learn how one mind speaks to another beyond words and in silence. He must learn to listen 'with the third ear'". (Reik, 1948, p. 144)

We evoke this usage of 'reflection' and its cognates in such statements as, "The whole interview reflected a callous indifference typical of that firm"; or, "The Prime Minister's statement reflected her moralistic political style"; or, "Those dentures reflect the deft hand of Dr. Jones"; or, using other verbs, "Sever Hall in Harvard Yard is a typical Richardson design"; or, "That particular set of vocal exercises is indicative of the Husler Technique". The idea is not so much that one can recognise the hand, mind, or heart *behind* the achievement (though that too is possible) as that one recognises the *signature of* the achievement, what individuates it as an achievement among similar others.

As a dimension of the aesthetics of learning, the recognition of signature and style in the accomplishments (or failures, for that matter) of others represents a phase of maturity in the growth of understanding and an important source of further knowledge. Following my strategy up to now, I want to examine the symbolic conditions of style and signature recognition in learning.

Reflection, Style, and Signature

Yet another anecdote, this time of a personal style of teaching, often recognisable by the learner only long after having undergone it. I recall one such experience from my adolescence—typical, I'm sure, of many similar experiences in the classroom, on the job, or on the playing field. This one happened to occur in the music studio.

I was fourteen and having trouble understanding my voice teacher, Mr. Rupert Nieley's concept of the "Ah-point": his jargon for inspanning the pharanx with a raised glottis—the yawn reflex so crucial to what singers call an "open throat". I simply could not get it try as I might time and time again. "Ah!, Vernon, Ah! Ah!" he boomed forth with gestures suggesting that his own throat was a virtual chasm. All I could manage was a thin, little nasal "a" as in "at". Suddenly I stopped in frustration and blurted out, "Mr. Nieley, I just don't seem to be getting anywhere. I can't find my Ah-point!" Mr. Nieley paused at the keyboard giving me a long hard look from under his shock of white hair. Resting his hands on the piano lyre, he quietly asked, "Vernon, why are you here?" "To . . . to learn how to sing, Mr. Nieley", I stammered. "I mean, really why are you here?" he retorted. "Why do you want to sing? Why do you and little Jimmie Genovese and all the others come here week after week?" I was stunned by the question, at a complete loss. "I don't know, Mr. Nieley". "Yes you do, Vernon, you just haven't realised it yet. Those great voices—Caruso, McCormack, Bjoerling, Merrill, Tucker, even Lanza—have captured your imagination; and so you and Jimmie and the others come here because you want Culture. *Culture*, Vernon", he added for emphasis. "Culture is what you seek, and the Ah-point is but one step along the way". This was a lot for me then to grasp, but I somehow sensed with my "third ear" more than knew that something wonderfully important had been revealed to me beyond my admiration of great singers and the desire to sing myself. It was not until years later, long after Mr. Nieley's death, that I fully understood what he meant and, in fact, agreed with the diagnosis. Even then, his remarks that day wholly (if vaguely) transformed my vision of what I was trying to do: something I knew not quite what, something touching upon my entire future, was at stake far more significant than just the Ah-point—which, as it happened, came in its own good time.

Mr. Nieley, though a fine vocal technician, always kept a note of prophecy in reserve for such moments of distress as described above. He had an acute sense of when to deliver such "philosophical" observations so as to shape the character, inform, and distract the learner from vexation. I now see this as his signature as a teacher, as indicative of his style of teaching, indeed of a style of teaching whether of singing or anything else. Many's the time over the years I've caught myself thinking, There's the Nieley imprint at work (in myself), or, There's a Nieley-like approach (in others). "Not to detect a man's style", Michael Oakshott reminds us, "is to have missed three-quarters of the meaning of his actions and utterances; and not to have acquired a style is to have shut oneself off from the ability to convey any but the crudest meanings". (Oakshott, 1967, p. 169)[7]

But what are style and signature in this connection? What are we to make of such notions normally associated with works of art and ·art criticism when applied to ordinary work? Mr. Nieley's teaching efforts, though perhaps artful and aimed at mastery of an art form, were not themselves art any more than Dewey's job interview, however artfully conducted, was art. Yet we should be far quicker to admit talk of style than of "aesthetics" when discussing such matters. We routinely speak of style (individual or institutional) in professions like business, politics, medicine, law; in crafts and trades like carpentry, ship building, or cooking; in industrial design and technology; and, of course, in clothing or a person's manner of comportment ("That's his style, to avoid rather than confront the issue"). The question, again, is what literal sense, if any, can be made of such talk?

Symbolism, Style, and Signature

Some passing remarks of Goodman on style and signature in art suggest a tentative line of analysis. Goodman asks, "what in general distinguishes stylistic features from others?" Such features include many symbolic functions of art: ways of saying, exemplifying, or expressing. However, "a property—whether of statement made, structure displayed, or feeling conveyed— counts as stylistic", says Goodman, "only when it associates a work with one rather than another artist, period, region, school, etc. A style is a complex characteristic that serves somewhat as an individual or group signature . . . but in general stylistic properties help answer the questions: who? when? where?" (Goodman, 1978, p. 34) Then, in a brief passage, Goodman raises the very point at issue here: "Throughout, I have been speaking of style of works of art. But need style, as conceived here, be confined to works, or might the term 'work' in our definition be as well replaced by 'object' or by 'anything'?" (p. 35)

His answer is that "What counts are properties symbolized, whether or not the artist chose or is even aware of them; and many things other than works of art symbolize". (p. 36) So, a basic condition of something's having style is that it symbolises in ways bearing upon the questions, who? when? where? "Natural objects and events", says Goodman, "may function otherwise as symbols, and properties of what they symbolize may be characteristic of time or place of origin or occurrence. A Mandalay sunrise may be not merely a sunrise in Mandalay but a sunrise expressing the suddenness of thunder—a sunrise in Mandalay style". (p. 36) Similarly, a sea-landscape may be in Bay of Fundy or Cape Cod style, a weathered stone in the style of Brancusi, a mottled paint spill in the style of a Pollock. [8]

Yet if Who? When? Where? will do for works of art, What? How? and Why? may have to be added for work where style also encompasses the selection of tasks undertaken, the techniques employed, and their rationales. Quite possibly, because of the relative "opacity" of works of art (See p. 142 above), style may be more narrowly circumscribed in art than elsewhere. But that is a topic I leave for another time.

With whatever considerations in mind, such recognition of style in art or anywhere is no simple reading off of parallels and similarities given even if they are *there*, as it were, for the taking. Rather, learning by reflection on the style of things, people, or events is a matter of what we are *equipped* by prior experience and training to comprehend, what we are *prepared* to notice, compare, assess, or discover.

In virtually any field or discipline, it requires a "reflective practitioner" to pick up on details of style.[9] "The style of Haydn or Hardy or Holbein", says Goodman, "does not proclaim itself to the casual listener or reader or museum goer, and is seldom to be recognized by following explicit instructions. Styles are normally accessible only to the knowing eye or ear, the tuned sensibility, the informed and inquisitive mind . . . What we find, or succeed in making, is heavily dependent on how and what we seek". (p. 39) Similarly, what a "non-artistic" thing, event, person, or situation reflects in the way of style depends upon what we correctly or incorrectly read into or out of it, with what questions in mind, by whatever symbolic means at our disposal.

Writing in quite another vein, Theodor Reik again makes a parallel point about the psychoanalyst's reflections upon patient behaviour. "It can be demonstrated that the analyst, like his patient, knows things without knowing that he knows them. The voice that speaks in him, speaks low, but he who listens with the third ear hears also what is expressed almost noiselessly, what is said *pianissimo*". What is more, "Those unconscious feelers are not there to master a problem, but to search for it". (Reik, 1948, p. 145)[10]

This brings us to a fundamental point about reflection on style. Style, however detected or defined, is a suggestive as well as complex quality, an invitation to exploration based on what Wittgenstein calls, "imponderable evidence" including "subtleties of glance, of gesture, of tone". (Wittgenstein, 1953, p. 228; on the eventual ponderability of imponderable evidence, see Howard, 1982, pp. 63-65) Like true love, style is more readily felt and perceived than explained, except in retrospect.

The teaching style, for example, of a Fagan, a Mr. Chips, or a Mr. Nieley is not readily reducible to some specifiable quirk or simple "method" or fixed list of qualities. "A complex and subtle style", says Goodman, "like a trenchant metaphor, resists reduction to a literal formula". (Goodman, 1978, p. 40) The more complex the style, the more we are forced to reflect upon it with little or no hope of specifying its necessary and sufficient conditions. Nor should we care to (unless we are in a simplistic mood) for that would be to foreclose further understanding of the powerful example and personal imprint of the Mr. Nieleys in our lives.

Reflections on a Hydrangea

The hydrangea is a typically late blooming shrub in the far north temperate zone, coming to flower slowly in August and lasting well into September. Hardy and sometimes achieving great age, it requires little attention once established. Reaching a height of about ten feet at maturity, its white, pink, or pale blue blossoms cluster like pompoms in a great canopy of colour. Remarkably resistent to infestations, it is a reliable plant, stately in its way and symmetrical, and seldom disappointing in its natural growth. The hydrangea is a self-contained, unpretentious, yet commanding plant. Its pastel colours in full bloom are difficult to ignore. So one should take care where to place it on any cultivated landscape.

Schiller in his eighth *Letter* says, "It is . . . not enough to say that all intellectual enlightenment deserves our respect only insofar as it reacts upon the character; to a certain extent it proceeds from the character, since the way to the head must lie through the heart. Training of the sensibility is then the more pressing need of our age, not merely because it will be a means of making the improved understanding effective for living, but for the very reason that it awakens this improvement". (Schiller, 1795, p. 50)

Nearly everything contained in these pages, about imagination, expression, and learning by instruction, practice, example, and reflection, has been a variation on the theme of cultivating the sensibilities as a neglected aspect of cognitive growth; that is to say, as a neglected aspect of learning *theory*. It is we who try to "explain" learning—psychologists and philosophers—who trip over our cherished abstractions and loose our grip on the nub of the matter. Practitioners, even if unaware of their own sensibilities, have them and use them. Primarily, it is educational planners and theorists whom I should like to see become more "Schillerian" in their outlook.

Unlike Peters, I do not construe such training of the sensibilities as an "education of the emotions" *per se*. (Peters, 1972) Nor, like Dewey, do I see such training as simple as taking account of the "emotional quality" of learning. (See p. 135 above) Nor, like Read, do I consider such training mostly a childhood affair that will take care of itself once instilled. (See p. 136 above) Rather, an education of the sensibilities appropriate to any domain, at any stage of development, is a kind of continuing "aesthetic education"—a learning by all means—drawing upon the whole range of perceptual and symbolic capacities that our culture and its many sub-worlds bequeaths to us, and which capacities we need to do as well as we can. As learners, we should be so lucky as to grow like a hydrangea.

Notes

1 The novels of C. P. Snow, particularly his eleven-volume series, *Strangers and Brothers* (1985), come to mind as exploring the day to day drama of professional life in science, education, and politics.

2 For Dewey, "Experience occurs continuously, because of the interaction of live creature and environing conditions in the very process of living". (1934, p. 35) Within that flow, he contrasts the "humdrum" of passive experience, suspended between the extremes of loose ends and rigid habit, with "an experience"—something which stands out, "because marked out from what went before and what came after". (1934, pp. 36 and 40) More on that below.

3 For a shrewd account of philosophical and psychological perspectives on how conceptualisation influences observational data, see Israel Scheffler's *Science and Subjectivity*, 2nd edition (1982), Chapter 2, "Observation and Objectivity", pp. 21-44.

4 A recent study of school administration congenial to the "aesthetic" approach to learning taken herein is Arthur Blumberg's *School Administration as a Craft* (Needham Heights: Allyn & Bacon, 1989). Quite incidentally, Blumberg also begins by following Wittgenstein's "nose" as I discovered, much to my amusement, after being well along in the present study.

5 Concerning Dewey's *magnum opus* on reflective thought, *How We Think* (1933), and ignoring the many valuable insights to be gleaned from that work, I agree with Richard Rorty's assessment in his introductory essay to the latest edition that, "What Dewey describes as 'reflective thinking' sometimes sounds like something everybody does quite naturally, something which is the common property of the ancients and the moderns, and of any reasonably literate and articulate person, no matter what his or her persuasion. But sometimes, particularly when Dewey is comparing this sort of thinking invidiously with 'intellectualism' and 'rationalism', reflective thinking sounds like something quite particular, something which the moderns do more of than the ancients did, something more commonly found among laboratory scientists than among medieval school men, and more prevalent among liberals than among conservatives". (Rorty, 1986, Introduction to Dewey, 1933, p. xiii) In short, Dewey's treatment of reflective thinking is ambiguous between how, *de facto*, we think reflectively and how, *de jure*, we ought to. Other-

wise said, Dewey seems mostly concerned to promote his own version of post-seventeenth century "scientific method" as an all-purpose "better way of thinking". (Dewey, 1933, p. 113)

6   I have nothing in mind like a meta-language in logic or second-order conceptual analysis. The simple idea of "rehashing" an issue comes closer to the mark. Nor do I assume that *thought*, as such begins with reflection; for as James observes in his famous chapter on "The Stream of Thought" in the *Principles of Psychology* (1980), "*The first fact for us . . . as psychologists, is that thinking of some sort goes on . . .* If we could say in English 'it thinks', as we say 'it rains' or 'it blows', we should be stating the fact most simply and with the minimum of assumption. As we cannot, we must simply say that *thought goes on*". (pp. 219-220; italics his) Peirce similarly remarks on the "continuous stream" of consciousness in his "Some Consequences of Four Incapacities" (1868) suggesting that "just as we say that a body is in motion, and not that motion is in a body we ought to say that we are in thought, and not that thoughts are in us". (p. 236, fn)

7   Oakshott also tells a tale of style-detection not unlike my own. " . . . if you were to ask me the circumstances in which patience, accuracy, economy, elegance and style first dawned upon me, I would have to say that I did not come to recognize them in literature, in argument or in geometrical proof until I had first recognized them elsewhere; and that I owed this recognition to a Sergeant gymnastics instructor who lived long before the days of 'physical education' and for whom gymnastics was an intellectual art—and I owed it to him, not on account of anything he ever said, but because he was a man of patience, accuracy, economy, elegance and style". (Oakshott, 1967, p. 176)

8   Coincidentally, I recently ran across this passage in John Le Carré's *A Murder of Quality* (1964). "Smiley? Ah! You've met True, have you—Miss Truebody, my housekeeper? Marvelous this snow, isn't it? Pure Bruegel! Seen the boys skating by the Eyot? Marvelous sight! Black suits, coloured scarves, pale sun; all there, isn't it, all there! Bruegel to the life. Marvelous!" (p. 47)

9   Cf. Donald A. Schon, *The Reflective Practitioner* (New York: Basic Books, 1983). Schon's work on the reform of design education is closely kindred to the overall approach to learning taken herein. See also his, "The Design Process", in *Varieties of Thinking, Essays From Harvard's Philosophy of Education Research Centre*, ed. V. A. Howard, (New York: Routledge, Chapman & Hall, 1990).

10 Reik deserves quotation at length on the psychological side of these ever so elusive patterns of exemplification. "Nothing can, of course, be said about the nature of those unconscious impressions we receive as long as they remain unconscious. Here are a few representative instances of

some that become conscious. They concern the manner, not the manners, of persons who were in the process of psychoanalysis, little peculiarities, scarcely noticed movements, intonations, and glances that might otherwise have escaped conscious observation because they were inconspicuous parts of the person's behaviour. People generally tend to brush aside observations of this sort as immaterial and inconsequential, little things not worthy of our attention". (Reik, 1948, p. 148) Better examples of aesthetic sensibility at work to further learning and understanding would be difficult to find.

References

Arthur Blumberg, *School Administration as a Craft* (Needham Heights: Allyn & Bacon, 1989).

Jerome Bruner, "Value and Need as Organizing Factors in Perception" (1947), reprinted in Jeremy M. Anglin, ed., *Beyond the Information Given* (New York: W. W. Norton, 1973).

John Dewey, *Democracy and Education* (New York: Macmillan, 1966); first published in 1916.

John Dewey, *How We Think: A Restatement of the Relation of Reflective Thinking to the Educative Process* (Carbondale: University of Southern Illinois Press, 1986); first published in 1933.

John Dewey, *Art as Experience* (New York: Putnam, 1958); first published in 1934.

Nelson Goodman, *Languages of Art, An Approach to a Theory of Symbols* (Indianapolis: Hackett, 1972).

Nelson Goodman, "When is Art?", in *Ways of Worldmaking* (Indianapolis: Hackett, 1978).

Nelson Goodman, "The Status of Style", in *Ways of Worldmaking* (Indianapolis: Hackett, 1978).

V. A. Howard, *Artistry: the Work of Artists* (Indianapolis: Hackett, 1982).

William James, *The Principles of Psychology* (Cambridge: Harvard University Press, 1983); first published in 1890.

Immanuel Kant, *Critique of Pure Reason* (1781), tr. Norman Kemp Smith, first ed. (A), second ed. (B), (London: Macmillan, 1958).

Immanuel Kant, *Critique of Judgement* (1790), tr. J. C. Meredith (Oxford: Oxford University Press, 1952).

John Le Carr¨, *A Murder of Quality* (London: Penguin, 1964).

Michael Oakshott, "Learning and Teaching", in R. S. Peters, ed., *The Concept of Education* (London: Routledge & Kegan Paul, 1967).

C. S. Peirce, "Some Consequences of Four Incapacities", *Journal of Speculative Philosophy* (1868); reprinted in Justus Buchler, ed., *Philosophical Writings of Peirce* (New York: Dover, 1955).

R. S. Peters, "The Education of the Emotions", in R. F. Dearden, P. H. Hirst, R. S. Peters, eds., *Education and the Development of Reason* (London: Routledge & Kegan Paul, 1972).

Herbert Read, *Education Through Art*, 2nd edition (London: Farber & Farber, 1945).

Theodor Reik, *Listening With the Third Ear* (New York: Farrar, Straus & Giroux, 1948).

Richard Rorty, Introduction to John Dewey, *How We Think* (Carbondale: University of Southern Illinois Press, 1986).

Israel Scheffler, "In Praise of the Cognitive Emotions", *Teachers College Record*, vol. 79, 1977; reprinted in Israel Scheffler, *Inquiries, Philosophical Studies of Language, Science, and Learning* (Indianapolis: Hackett, 1986).

Israel Scheffler, *Science and Subjectivity*, 2nd edition, (Indianapolis: Hackett, 1982).

Friedrich von Schiller, *On the Aesthetic Education of Man, in a Series of Letters* (1795), tr. Reginald Snell (New York: Frederick Unger, 1965).

Donald A. Schon, *The Reflective Practitioner* (New York: Basic Books, 1983).

Donald A. Schon, "The Design Process", in V. A. Howard, ed., *Varieties of Thinking, Essays From Harvard's Philosophy of Education Research Centre* (New York: Routledge, Chapman & Hall, in press).

Roger Scruton, *Kant* (Oxford: Oxford University Press, 1982).

C. P. Snow, *Strangers and Brothers*, eleven volumes, 1949-1970 (New York: Scribners, 1985); in three volumes.

Ludwig Wittgenstein, *Philosophical Investigations*, tr., G. E. M. Anscombe (Oxford: Blackwell, 1976); first published in 1953.

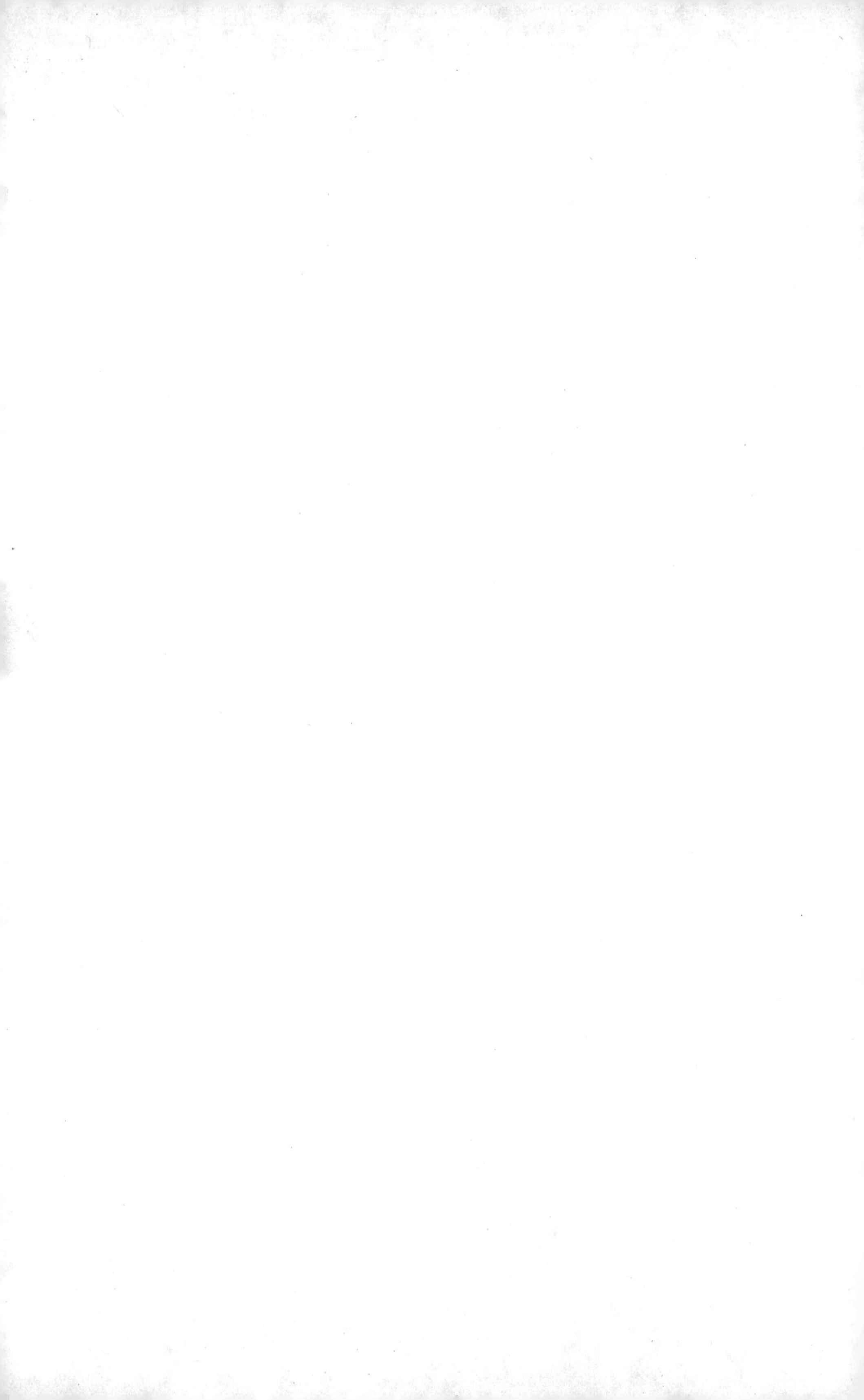